I

PIRATE AND MERMAID[1]

*Some years ago a tall tower stood at the extreme end
of Cape Marabata; the Christians called it Torre
Blanquilla (White Tower) and it was known to the
Mohammedans as El-Minar. All day long the tower
looked out on the sea; at night it was lulled to sleep by
the murmur of the wind on the water. It was an
ancient tower whose walls were covered with gnarled
vines; scorpions hid between her stones, and evil jinn
gathered nearby at nightfall. The gypsies, who knew
about all things, said the tower was built by the
Portuguese who came here to fight against the
Mohammedans. The mountaineers of Andjera are
better informed; they say the tower was built by Lass
el-Behar the pirate in order to hide his treasures within its walls.*

*Lass el-Behar came from Rabat. He was a skill-
ful navigator, and skilled at an even more difficult
art — that of commanding men. The Spaniards and
Italians knew his name only too well. El-Behar's
frigate was slender and light as a swallow; the oars of*

---

1. "The Legend of El-Minar." Chimenti (1965)

7

a hundred Christian galley slaves made it skim swiftly over the waves. The ship was greatly feared because of the boldness of her sailors and her many cannons, each different from the other, which the pirate had captured from Christian vessels of various nationalities.

Lass el-Behar was young, handsome, and brave. Many a captive Christian woman fell deeply in love with him, as did the daughters of rich and powerful Mohammedans. But he rejected the love of Christians and Mohammedans alike, for his ship meant far more to him than the beauty of women. He loved his ship, the companionship of his valiant warriors, and the glorious battles which were later to be celebrated in song and poetry. Above all it was the sea he loved; he loved her with so deep a passion that he could not live away from her, and he spoke to her as men speak to their sweethearts. His warriors would say that at the hour of prayer he would turn his eyes away from the direction of Mecca in order to gaze at the sea.

On the day of Aid el-Kbir (sheep sacrifice), Lass el-Behar, who was in the village of El-Minar with his companions-in-arms, declined to go to Tangier to hear the sermon of the cadi and to pray in the company of the devout.

"Go if you must," he said to his men. "As for me I shall rest here."

He shut himself up in his tower; from there he could contemplate the sea and the ships as they moved slowly on the horizon. The charqui, more breeze than wind, made the water dance under the warm summer light.

"The best sermon of the cadi," thought el-Behar, "could never equal the beauty of this scene. What

prayer, be it ever so perfect, could equal the sweet murmur of rippling waters? What on earth is as powerful as the sea which stretches from one shore of the world to the other? Oh, would that the waves were a woman so that I might marry her and the ocean a mosque in which I might pray."

As these thoughts were running through his mind a storm gathered in the west; it swept over the plains and the mountains and roared about the tower. The sea gulls cried out in fright and flew away; flocks of sheep ran frantically to their enclosures. The tempest lasted a day and a night.

When the wind quieted down and the sea ceased to bellow like a thousand oxen, Lass el-Behar descended from his tower. On the narrow band of sand which lay between the rocks and the water he saw a woman lying stretched out, white and cold. He approached closer.

"She must be a Christian," he said to himself, "for her hair is the color of new gold."

He lifted her up and took her in his arms.

"Perhaps she is still alive."

The woman opened her eyes; they were green eyes, green as the algae which grows in the cracks of rocks. She was a bahria, a jinniyeh (female genie) of the sea. Her beauty was magic and el-Behar fell madly in love with her. He neglected his warriors for her sake; he forgot his swift galley, his glory, and even his prayers to Allah.

"I love you more than anything on earth," he once said to her, "more than my life and my salvation."

During the equinox, the furious sea again hammered at the tower and threatened the village nearby.

9

Her waters mingled with those of the Charf River and even reached the garden of Tanger el-Balia.

"The ocean is going to smash our tower," said the pirate to his beloved, "let us flee to the mountains."

"Why fear the ocean?" asked the bahria with a smile. "Don't you love her above all things? Aren't you constantly praising her force and her power? Don't you turn your head away from the direction of Mecca in order to gaze out at the sea? I am a daughter of the sea. I came to reward you for the love you bear her. Now the sea calls me back. Farewell, Lass el-Behar, you shall never see me again."

"Don't leave me," implored the pirate, "don't leave me, I beg of you. Without you I shall never know happiness."

"Happiness," answered the bahria, "belongs only to those who fear Allah and honor Him. I must leave you. I dare not disobey the voice which calls me, but you may follow me if you wish."

The jinniyeh wandered off with the tide and Lass el-Behar followed her into the murky depths of the sea. Nor was he ever seen again. He sleeps under the waves between the Tarik Mountain (Gibraltar) and Cape Tres-Forcas. He will not waken until that day when men will be judged for their actions and the earth will only be a shadow of a shadow which will finally disappear.

For Allah is the Almighty One.

II

A CHRISTIAN TURN'D TURKE

"Christians are made Turks and Turks are the sons of devils."
—*Newwes from Sea of WARD THE PIRATE* (1609)

From about the late 1500's to the 18th century, many thousands of European men—and women—converted to Islam. Most of them lived and worked in Algiers, Tunis, Tripoli, and the Rabat-Salé area of Morocco—the so-called Barbary Coast States. Most of the women became Moslems when they married Moslem men. This much is easy enough to understand, although it would be fascinating if we could trace the lives of some of them in search of some 17th century Isabelle Eberhardt.[2] But what about the men? What caused *them* to convert?

Christian Europeans had a special term for these men: *Renegadoes*, "renegades": apostates, turncoats, traitors. Christians had some reason for these sentiments, since Christian Europe was still at war with Islam. The Crusades had never really ended. The last Moorish kingdom in Spain,

---

2. Isabelle Eberhardt, daughter of Russian anarchists, traveled and lived in Algiers, sometimes dressed and passed as a man, converted to Islam, and supported Algerian independence. She wrote romantically about her bizarre and erotic adventures and died young and tragically. See Bowles (1975) and de Voogd (1987).

Grenada, was added to the Reconquista only in 1492, and the last Moorish uprising in Spain took place in 1610. The Ottoman Empire, vigorous, brilliant, and armed to the teeth (just like its contemporary Elizabethan/Jacobean England), pressed its offensive against Europe on two fronts, by land toward Vienna, and by sea westward through the Mediterranean.

In the vernacular languages of Europe, "Turk" meant any Muslim, including the Moors of North Africa. The Renegadoes were said to have "Turn'd Turke" (the title of a play, *A Christian turn'd Turke* by Robert Daborne, performed in London in 1612). [Ewen, 1939: 3; Lloyd, 1981: 48. According to Lloyd, the playwright's name was Robert Osbourne.] The Lusty Turk and the Wicked Soldier populated popular literature—and "mussulmano!" is *still* a deadly insult in Venice. One might understand a tiny bit of this European ignorance and prejudice by thinking of the American media during the recent Gulf War with Iraq. Europe's response to Islam since the 19th century has become far more complex, because 19th century Europe actually conquered and colonized much of *Dar al-Islam*. But in the 17th century there existed no such point of interpenetration of cultures, however one-sided. For the most part, Europe hated and misunderstood Islam. As for Islam, the word *jihad*, Holy War, sums up its attitude toward Christendom. Tolerance and understanding were almost non-existent on both sides of the cultural divide.

The Renegadoes therefore seemed like creatures of hellish mystery to most Europeans. Not only had they "betrayed Our Lord," they had gone even farther and joined the *jihad* itself. Almost to a man, the Renegadoes were employed as "Barbary Corsairs". They attacked and looted European ships and ravished Christian captives back to Barbary, to be ransomed or sold as slaves. Of course Christian "Corsairs",

including the Knights of Malta, were doing exactly the same thing to the ships and crews of Moslem vessels. But very few of the Moslem captives "turned Christian". The flow of renegades went largely one way.

Europeans assumed that the apostates were human scum, and believed that their motives for conversion were the lowest imaginable: greed, resentment, revenge. Many of them were already "pirates" when they converted—obviously they simply wanted an excuse for more piracy. Of course, some of them were captured and offered a choice of conversion or slavery. But like cowards, they chose apostasy and crime.[3] Renegadoes were slain on sight in all European countries and burnt to death in Spain (at least in theory), even if they wanted to re-convert. In this sense Islam was seen as a kind of moral plague, rather than simply an enemy ideology.

Within Islamdom the attitude toward conversion can be described as more open. The Spanish forced Jews and Moslems to convert, but then expelled them anyway. Islam however still retained an image of itself as a new religion, seeking to expand by all possible means, and especially by conversion. "New Muslims" are still considered blessed and even "lucky", especially on the frontiers of Islam. These differing attitudes toward the act of conversion help to explain

3. Clearly at least some of the Renegadoes were quite eager to convert. An arrogant French Consul to Algiers (1731–2) named Leon Delane, "who had previously served as French consul in Candia (Crete) and had caused much trouble by his haughtiness and scorn for the Turks, interfered with the attempt by a sailor from St. Tropez to turn renegade, although the treaty between the two states specifically stated (Article 19) that if a Frenchman persisted for three consecutive days in his intention to turn Muslim he should be so recognized." Delane was transferred back to Crete by an embarrassed French government [Spencer, 1976: 159].

how more Christians turn'd Turke than vice versa—but the question "why?" remains unanswered.[4] Perhaps we can begin by assuming that neither the Christian nor the "Turkish" interpretation of the Renegadoes can satisfy our curiosity. We may doubt, on the one hand, that these men were all simply demonic, and, on the other, that they were all angels of the *jihad*. We can assume that our answers—if any prove possible—will seem far more *complex* than either of these 17th-century theories.

Curiously enough, it appears that few modern historians have really tried to understand the Renegadoes. Among European historians the effect of the "demon theory" still lingers, although it has been rationalized and elaborated and even inverted into a plausible-sounding hypothesis. The reasoning goes something like this: How did the great European powers fail to eradicate the Barbary corsairs for *three whole centuries?* It goes without saying that Islamic military and naval technology was inferior to European. Moslems, as everyone knows, make bad sailors. How to explain this apparent conundrum? Obviously—the Renegadoes. They, as *Europeans*, introduced European technology to the Moslems, and fought for them as well. It appears therefore that Barbary piracy was *"une affaire des étrangers"*; without the Renegadoes it could never have happened [Coindreau, 1948]. They were traitors of the worst sort—but brilliant in their crude and thuggish way. Piracy is despicable—but, after all, a bit romantic!

---

4. One Captain Hamilton explained the motive which induced some Renegadoes to stay on in Barbary: "They are tempted to forsake their God for the love of Turkish [i.e., Moslem] women who are generally very beautiful." He forgave the poor wretches their weakness, for these women "are well versed in witchcraft...captives never get free." [Wolfe, 1979: 237]

As for Islamic historians, they naturally resent any suggestions of Islamic inferiority. The 19th and early 20th century local histories of Rabat-Salé, for example, make it quite clear that the Moors, Berbers and Arabs of the country contributed, in the long run, far more to the history of the "holy war at sea" than did a few thousand converts. As for the converts themselves, their descendants still live in Rabat-Salé—they *became Moroccans*, whatever their origins. The history of the corsairs is not "an affair of foreigners", but part of the history of the Maghreb, the Far West of Islam, and of the emerging Moroccan nation [Hesperis, 1971].

None of these "explanations" of the Renegadoes gets us any closer to their possible motives for embracing Islam along with the life of the Barbary corsairs. Brilliant traitors or assimilated heroes—neither stereotype possesses any real depth. Both contain elements of truth. The pirates did introduce certain technical and strategic novelties to Barbary, as we shall see. And they did participate in Islam in more complex ways than simply as hired thugs—or "experts"—as we shall also see. But we still have no inkling of the *"why?"* of the whole phenomenon. We should note at once that although some of the Renegadoes were literate in numerous languages, none were *literati*. We have no firsthand accounts, no texts by Renegadoes. Their social origins did not dispose them to self-analytical writing; that luxury was still a monopoly of the aristocracy and emerging middle class. The pen of history is in the hand of the enemies of the Renegadoes; they themselves are silent.

Thus we may never be able to uncover their motives. Perhaps we can do no more than suggest a number of complex and even contradictory impressions and speculations. But we can still do better than the neocolonialist Euro-historians, or the Moroccan nationalists, who both see the Renegadoes only in relation to their own ideological precon-

ceptions. We can try to appreciate the Renegadoes for themselves, as individuals (if possible) and as a group, with their own interests and agendas, their own values, their own self-image. We can attempt to see (as clearly as the evidence allows) from *inside* the phenomenon, rather than depend on the light of outside interpretations.

To focus attention on a *specific history* (or "microhistory", as C. Ginzberg put it) might help us to refine our perceptions of the Renegadoes more easily than if we attempted a global view of the entire phenomenon.[5] The methodology used here consists of reading historical/ethnographical texts in the light of "the History of Religions". I prefer to call this framework *histories of religion* however, for two reasons: First, to avoid the imputation that I adhere to the school of Eliade, which has almost monopolized the label "History of Religions" for itself. I use some of the categories developed by Eliade, also by Henry Corbin, but find them less useful in dealing with concepts such as "resistance" or "insurrectionary desire". Which leads to the second reason for preferring the term *histories of religion*: any academic discipline which calls itself The History of anything whatsoever must be suspected *a priori* of erecting a false *totality* based on dubious absolutes which will serve only to mask and reinforce the ideologies of elites. Therefore the third chief methodological ingredient of this essay derives from a Nietzschean history of ideas, images, emotions, aesthetic signs, etc., as developed by G. Bachelard, W. Benjamin, G. Bataille, M. Foucault, etc. — an historical discipline which begins by questioning and criticizing the absoluteness of *History* as anything other than an *idea* with a

---

5. This essay will not constitute a genuine microhistory because it is based largely on secondary sources. I simply wish to express a methodological debt to Ginzberg and his school, without claiming in any way to match them for rigor and originality.

history of its own. And finally, the chief methodological tool here is really *piratology*, which—as everyone knows—is exclusively the province of enthusiastic amateurs.

So we'll center our study around one community in one brief period (about 50 years): Rabat-Salé, in the first half of the 17th century. Of all the Barbary states, Salé was the only one in which the corsairs achieved independence. Algiers, Tunis, and Tripoli were all protectorates of the Sublime Porte, but Salé—for a few decades—was governed by a "divan" or Council of Corsair Captains. It was a true "pirate utopia", and thus we can hope to find the Renegado in his most evolved form, his most sophisticated political and spiritual state of development, here in the "Republic of Bou Regreg", the "Moorish" or "Corsair Republic of Salé".

First, however, we can also try something which none of the historians (as far as I know) has yet done for the Renegadoes. We can ask if Europe really was monolithically opposed to Islam. We can ask if Islam possessed a *positive shadow*, so to speak, which might have hidden itself within European culture, and might have influenced the Renegadoes *even before* their escape to Barbary. We might give them the benefit of the doubt, and not simply assume that their motives for conversion were all base and empty of real significance. We might wonder if Islam itself (and not just the hope of pirate gold) could have attracted them to North Africa—or, if not "Islam itself", then some image or rumor or myth or misconception of Islam. In what way, then, might a 17th century working–class mariner have acquired an interest in or even an attraction toward Islam?

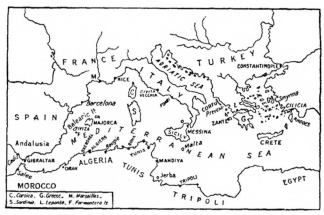

THE MEDITERRANEAN, SHOWING THE MAIN BARBARY BASES

At the time of the Crusades the idea of an "esoteric Islam" began to sift back to Europe along with all the spices and silks—and books—the holy warriors of Christ managed to "liberate" from the Holy Land. Did the Ismaili "Assassins" pass along some secret knowledge to the Templars? And is this why the Templars were proscribed, tortured, executed, extirpated with such seemingly insane hatred? Were alchemy and neoplatonism passed along through Moorish Spain to the rest of Europe, especially Italy and France? Did St. Francis and Roger Bacon and other mystical missionaries to the Saracens bring back with them some elements of Islamic gnosis, hermetic science, and Sufism?

In any case, whether these contacts really occurred or not, by the beginning of the 17th century some European intellectuals *believed* they had occurred, and that some real transmission of secret wisdom had in fact been carried out. (The reality or irreality of such contacts is a subject for

research; here we are concerned only with a history of *images*, of beliefs and ideas, which profoundly influence human society whether or not they are based in "historical reality".) The late Renaissance Hermeticists began to demonstrate a touch of Islamophilia. Around 1610 (the date of the last Moorish or "Morisco" revolt in Spain), some German occultists released a series of documents outlining the history of a secret order, the Rosicrucians. According to their account, the 14th-century founder of the Order, the probably-mythical Christian Rosenkreutz, had traveled widely in the Islamic world (Damascus, Arabia, a mythical city called Damcar, and the Moroccan city of Fez) and received there a complete course in Hermetic wisdom. His tomb, which had supposedly been recently re-discovered, contained enough coded illumination to make possible the revival of the Order. The Rosicrucian documents created a great stir among learned and pious Christians who had grown quite disgusted with the wars and quarrels of Catholicism and Protestantism, and yearned for a universal religion based on knowledge rather than faith. Islamic (and Jewish) science and wisdom were now eagerly desired for their contributions to this final Hermetic revelation. Publicly the Rosicrucians taught "tolerance even for Jews and Turks"; secretly they might have admitted that no one religion possessed the monopoly of truth. They remained Christians, but not "sectarians". Islam, for them, appears as simply another sect, in possession of some of the truth (including even certain truths about Jesus), but no more and no less limited than Catholicism or even Lutheranism. Thus, while the Rosicrucians did not convert to Islam, they exhibited far less hatred and intolerance for it than most Christians and even went so far as to praise it for its esoteric and occult traditions.

In a broader context, Islam might have had a sort of vague appeal for some Europeans who were simply anti-religious or

at least anti-clerical (along the lines, for instance, of the Elizabethan "School of Night", and Marlowe's quip that "Moses was a juggler"). A general impression of Islam's freedom from any authoritative priesthood or even dogma had percolated into European culture, or would soon do so. A long line of European intellectual Islamophiles began to appear. Rosicrucianism influenced Freemasonry which influenced the Enlightenment which influenced Nietzsche. Some of these tendencies and individuals actually knew something about Islam, but for the most part it was simply a matter of "the enemy of my enemy is my friend." Priests hate Islam; I hate priests; therefore I like Islam. Even in the 1880's Nietzsche's view of Islam was still rather two-dimensional—he seemed to see it as a sodality of aristocratic warrior monks—but his image of Islam was the culmination of a *tradition of free-thinkers* who viewed it primarily as a kind of *anti-Christianity*.

Hermeticism in turn influenced certain less-intellectual tendencies within Protestantism. Many of the extremists who were to carry out the English Revolution in the 1640's had been influenced by Jacob Boehme and other Hermetic-leaning Christian mystics. Even the working-class Levellers, Diggers, and Ranters had some acquaintance with Hermetic ideas and ideals—such as the esoteric interpretation of Scripture; universal tolerance; "pantheistic monism"; direct contact with the divine, without the intermediation of priest or Church; a tendency to antinomianism; a belief in the sacred quality of material Nature; an inclination to view "God" as "Universal Reason" (or *Mind*); faith in the power of the imagination to change reality; social egalitarianism; the millennium or "World Turn'd Upside Down"; etc.

No evidence suggests that any Ranter ever took an interest in Islam. However, there exists some reason to believe in connections between Ranterism and piracy. A "Ranter's Bay" in Madagascar sheltered a pirate utopia later in the 17th cen-

tury, and a number of Ranters were exiled to the Caribbean during the "Golden Age of Piracy" there. Certain aspects of Islamic thought might well appeal to extremist Protestants — such as anti-trinitarianism, the human but magical nature of Jesus, scriptural hermeneutics, "spiritual democracy", even the concept of Holy War. The Ranters (or other similar sects), who specialized in daring and outrageous spiritual paradox and antinominian extremism, might have had some influence on the kind of marginalized and rebellious men who were destined to end up in Algiers or Salé. [Besides the standard works by Hill (1978) and Cohn (1970), see Friedman (1987); Morton (1970); Smith (1983). For Ranter–Pirate connections see Hill (1985: 161-187).]

A ranter or proto-Ranter, who liked to "blaspheme gloriously" and preach in taverns while drinking and smoking, with a whore perched on his knee, might also have been attracted by the European image of Islam's *sensuality*. In effect Islam is a more pro-sexual religion than Christianity, and to some extent views pleasure as divine beneficence. The Koranic heavens of houris, cupbearers, gardens, and fountains of wine, have always been notorious among Christians dissatisfied with their own tradition's emphasis on chastity, virginity, and self-mortification. On the popular level the stereotype of the "Lusty Turk" preserved a caricature of this holy sensuality of Islam. The Orient began to be viewed (usually covertly) as a place where forbidden desires might be realized.

Finally, Islam was *the Enemy* of European Christian civilization. As M. Rediker (1987) has pointed out, by the 17th century the maritime world already revealed certain aspects of the Industrial Age which loomed so closely on the future's horizon. Ships were in some ways like floating factories, and maritime workers constituted a kind of proto-proletariat. Labor conditions in the merchant marines of Europe pre-

21

sented an abysmal picture of emerging capitalism at its worst—and conditions in European navies were even more horrendous. The sailor had every reason to consider himself the lowest and most rejected figure of all European economy and government—powerless, underpaid, brutalized, tortured, lost to scurvy and storms at sea, the virtual slave of wealthy merchants and ship-owners, and of penny-pinching kings and greedy princes. C. Hill and Rediker, basing themselves on earlier work by J. Lemisch, have both pointed out that in such a context, piracy must be studied as a form of *social resistance*. The pirate, who (in the words of one of Defoe's interviewees) "warred against all the world", was first and foremost the enemy of his own civilization. And once again, "the enemy of my enemy" just might prove to be my friend. I hate Europe. Europe hates Islam. Therefore…might I perhaps like Islam? What might a literate but not specially learned English reader know about Islam in, say, 1637? In that year an ambassador from the Moorish Corsair Republic of Salé visited London, and some professional journalist churned out a pamphlet on this marvel. He says,

> For their religion, they are strict observers of the law of Mahomet; they say Christ was a great Prophet, borne to bee a Saviour of the world (but not incarnate), that hee was the Breath of God, that hee was borne of a Virgin, and that the Jewes should have beleev'd in him, but would not; and therefore, because they went about to murder and crucifie him, he left them, and ascended from them into Heaven, and that then they put another man to death instead of him, whom they tormented and cruelly crucified. Therefore these

Mahometans doe hold and esteeme the Jewes as the worst of men, and very slaves to all nations of the world.

The one and onely booke of their religion is called their Alcaron, devised by their false prophet Mahomet, who was of their nation, a Larbee Arab. They may not use any other booke for devotion, nor, on paine of losse of life, no part of it doe they dare to examine or question; but if any be diffident, or any point or sentence be intricate and hard to be understood by any of them, then it is lawful to aske the meaning of the talby which is a poore weake-learned priest. They are all circumciz'd, and they use a kind of baptisme, but not in their churches, but at home in their houses.

Their Lent is much about the time as it is with us, which they doe hold but 30 dayes; but they neither eate nor drinke all the time on any of those dayes betwixt the dawning and the twilight, but when once the starres doe shew themselves, then, for their day fast, they feed fast all night. That priest or talby that cannot read over the booke of the Alcaron (or Mahomets Law) all over on their Good Friday at night is held unworthy of his place and function. They say their prayers six times every day and night, and they doe wash themselves all over very often. They have no bells to toll them to church, but he that is the clarke or sexton hath a deepe base great voyce, and goes to the top of the steeple, and there roares out a warning for the people to come to their devotions. No man doth enter their churches with

his shooes on. Their talbies or priests each one of them are allowed a wife or wives if they will. The lay-men may have captive women, but they must not lye with them in the night-time, for that belongs to the wives by turne, and, if any wife be beguiled of her turne, she may complaine for satisfaction to the magistrate. He that hath foure wives must be a rich man; a poore man is allowed as many, but his meanes are too short to keepe them; therefore one or two must serve his turne. The bride and bridegroome doe not see each other before the wedding-night that they are going to bed, where, if he finde her a maid, all is well; if otherwise, hee may turne her away and give her no part of the portion she brought him.

Their churchmen are not covetous or lovers of money or riches, for which cause they doe dayly in every towne and citty sit every day to heare and decide causes, which must be prooved by such witnesses as are not detected or knowne to be defamed for being drunkards, adulterers, prophaners, scandaliz'd persons, (for if they be knowne to be such, their testimony will not be taken). Likewise if the defendant can prove that the witnesse, which hath beene against him, hath not said his prayers six times duely in 24 houres, he or they shall utterly be disabled to beare witnesse, or give testimony in any cause whatsoever; but upon just and honest proofes the most tedious suite is ended in a weeke or eight daies at the most.

They are just in their words and promises;

for the which cause there is small use of bills, bonds, or obligations amongst them (which is the cause that there is scarce one rich scrivener either in Morocco, Fesse or Sus), for the breach of promise is held an unrecoverable disgrace amongst them. He that is taken with false weights or measures doth lose all his ware in his house to the use of the poore, and is a defamed person, and cruelly whipt. Their execution for life and death is that commonly the person adjudged to die hath his throat cut by the executioner.

Altogether an interesting mix of fact and fancy, and on the whole quite positive [*Sources Inédites*: 381–384]. We shall return to all these speculative themes and try to focus them more clearly in the specific context of the Corsair Republic of Salé. But before we can carry out such an operation we need to know more about the historical context of the Republic, and its chief economic resource — piracy. Specifically, we need to know more about the history of the whole Barbary Coast, and the Ottoman Protectorates of Algiers, Tunis and Tripoli.

"Torment of the Slaves", from *Histoire de Barbarie* (1637)

III

DEMOCRACY BY ASSASSINATION

"The Algerians are a company of rogues, and I am their captain."
— The Dey of Algiers to a European Consul[6]

Tunis, Tripoli, and especially Algiers, have been studied much more thoroughly than Salé; the interested reader will easily find an extensive bibliography—so it will not repay our time to devote too much detailed attention here to the Mediterranean coast states. Almost any book on pirate history will tell something about Algiers, and there are many works devoted exclusively to its history. Salé, which was smaller and more distant from the gaze of Europe, interests us not only because it's less well-known, but also because of its *political independence*. Even so, Salé was part of a "big picture" which we need to know at least in outline. The *Encyclopedia Britannica* (1953 edition), which doesn't even mention Salé in its entry on "Barbary Pirates", gives us this:

> The power of the piratical coast population of
> northern Africa arose in the 16th century,
> attained its greatest height in the 17th,

---

6. Spencer, 1976: 58

declined gradually throughout the 18th, and was extinguished only in the 19th century. From 1659 onwards the coast cities of Algeria and Tunisia, though nominally forming parts of the Turkish empire, were in fact anarchical military republics which chose their own rulers and lived by plunder. The maritime side of this long-lived brigandage was conducted by captains, or *reises*, who formed a class or even a corporation. Cruisers were fitted out by capitalists and commanded by the *reises*. The treasury of the pasha or his successors who bore the title of Agha or Dey or Bey, received 10% of the value of the prizes…. Until the 17th century the pirates used galleys, but Simon Danser, a Flemish renegade, taught them the advantages of using sailing ships. In the first half of the 17th century more than 20,000 captives were said to be imprisoned in Algiers alone. The rich were allowed to redeem themselves, but the poor were condemned to slavery. Their masters would not in many cases allow them to secure freedom by professing Mohammadanism. In the early part of the 19th century, Tripolitania, owing to its piratical practices, was several times involved in war with the United States. After the general pacification of 1815, the British made two vain attempts to suppress Algerian piracy, which was ended only by the French conquest of Algiers in 1830.

Note that Islam is called "Mohammadanism". Note that these piratical "Mohammadans" refused "in many cases" to permit conversion; the logical conclusion is that in *some* cases they *did* permit it—but the author prefers to avoid this conclusion, and to speak only in negative terms about mere "Mohammadans" and pirates.

Two interesting political terms are used here—"anarchical" and "capitalists"—which may not be quite appropriate. "Capitalist" sounds too 18–19th century to describe the merchants and ship-owning captains who fueled the economy of the corsair states. Moreover, I presume the author is not thinking of *anarchism* when he uses the term "anarchical" but is simply brandishing this word to indicate *violent disorder*. Algiers was subject to the Ottoman Empire, and thus could not have attained an anarchist form of organization in any strict sense of the word. As for the charge of "violent disorder", some scholars have asked how Algiers could have survived for centuries as a "corsair state" without some kind of internal continuity and stability. Earlier Eurocentric historians and sensationalist writers on piracy give us an impression of Algiers as a kind of ravening horde in a state of perpetual arousal; while more recent and less chauvinistic scholars like William Spencer (1976) tend to emphasize the stability of Algiers and to seek for possible explanations for its successful duration. The quasi-moralistic horror embedded in a term like "anarchical", as applied to North Africa, tends to obscure the secret fact that historians are frequently in the business of providing retrospective justifications for the imperialism and colonialism—the truly hideous rapacity—of 18–19th century Europe. If Algiers can be shown as a sinkhole of all decent human values, then we are permitted to go on believing in the "civilizing mission" of Europe's subsequent African and other colonial adventures. Hence the need for a massive *revising* of history as written by European (and

29

Euro-American) pseudo-rationalist apologists for piracy practiced by White Christian Nation States, as opposed to piracy practiced by mere Moorish "anarchicalists".[7]

In truth the government of Algiers seems to have been neither anarchical nor anarchist—but rather, in a strange and unexpected way, *democratic*. Unlike the European nations, gradually succumbing to the Absolutism of the Kings, Algiers exhibited signs of a more "horizontal" and egalitarian structure. In theory, of course, it was at all times subordinate to Turkish imperial policy and direction, but in practice the city-state was run by various "chambers" of Janissary soldiers and corsair notables, who made their own policy—and sometimes sent the Sultan's representatives scurrying back to Istanbul with a blunt refusal to carry out the will of the Sublime Porte.

To a certain extent the protectorates or "Regencies" of Algiers, Tunis, and Tripoli really were "affairs of foreigners", and perhaps might even be called quasi-colonies. In Algiers the *Ocak* or ruling body of Janissaries was made up—by law—not by natives of the regions (Moors, Arabs, Berbers) but rather by "Turks". But of course, as a further complication, the Janissary corps were originally not native

---

7. A useful term for the pirate enclaves—perhaps still not quite the *mot juste* — might be "ordered anarchy", originally applied by E. E. Evans-Pritchard to the tribal organization of the Nuer, and quoted by Richard Drinnon, who re-applies it to the "red-white republic of Fredonia" founded in Texas by the Cherokee chief Richard Fields and the fascinating John Dunn Hunter—a white who'd been captured by Indians as an infant, went to London where he met Robert Owen and other radicals, and returned to America in 1824. Hunter was another kind of Renegado—a convert to "Indianism"—and as such was hated and denounced. Fredonia failed and Hunter was murdered in 1827 [Drinnon, 1972: 208].

Anatolians or even born Moslems, but *slaves of the Sultan*, recruited as children under the Ottoman "boy tax" which operated in such outlying areas of the imperium as Christian Albania; they were trained, converted to Islam, and at first were used as the Ottoman equivalent of the Praetorian Guard. The Barbarossa brothers, who founded the Regency of Algiers, were Albanians or perhaps Greek Islanders by birth. They however received permission to begin recruiting native Anatolians into the Algerian branch of the corps, and eventually even European Renegadoes were admitted. The *Ocak*, like the knights of Saint John of Malta, comprised a military order in a holy war, and an occupying army, and a government, all in one. It seems that not one of the *Ocak* was ever born in North Africa—and in fact if a Janissary married a native woman and had children, these children were refused membership in the *Ocak* (a situation which led to several unsuccessful rebellions by such "half-breeds"). Native Algerians could and did rise to eminence and power—as *corsairs*—but never as military administrators. Hamida Reis, the last great 19th-century Algerian captain (Ar. *ra'is*), was a pure Kayble Berber. But in Algiers he was something of an exception. In any case, the "democracy" of the *Ocak* excluded native Algerians—and yet it also tended toward greater and greater independence from Turkey. If it was a "colony" of sorts, it was nevertheless only loosely connected to the homeland, unlike the later "*départements*" of the French. And the "Turks" always remained closer to the natives than any 19th-century European colonists by virtue of a shared religion. However much the Moors and Berbers may have hated the Turks, they joined forces with them when Spanish or French fleets loomed over the horizon.

We want to compare the government of Algiers with that of Salé, which was perhaps in part modeled on it. But the comparison of Algiers and Salé will have only a limited

usefulness for us precisely because of the former's Ottoman ties. Over the centuries Algiers absorbed a great deal of Turkish culture. The Janissaries were largely devoted to the Bektashi Sufi Order, a rather heterodox confraternity which sometimes used wine ritually, and exhibited many Turkic-shamanic features [Birge, 1937]. The famous Janissary marching music was originally a Sufi invention. Père Dan, a priest who came to Algiers in the 1630's to ransom captives and stayed on to produce an important history of the Regency, describes the investiture of Abd al-Hassan Ali in 1634 upon his arrival from Constantinople as the new triennial pasha:

> The city sent out two well-equipped galleys to do him honor. The officer corps of the Divan assembled in the number of five hundred to receive him at the port, where as he disembarked from his galley he was received with a salute of some fifteen hundred guns from the city forts and the corsair ships some forty of which came out under sail. There then marched the Agha of the Janissaries accompanied by two drummers (Cavus), followed by the Principal Secretary with the 24 Ayabashis who are the chief Counselors of State. There followed two by two the Bulukbashis with their huge plumed turbans, then the ranks of the Odabashis; there marched after them six Turkish oboists with Moors among them some playing flutes and other cymbals, the whole ensemble a very strange noise which aroused in us more fear than pleasure. Last came the new Pasha, enveloped as a mark of peace in a vast white robe. He rode a fine Barbary steed

32

richly harnessed with a silver bridle studded with gems, spurs and stirrups, reins of silk all laden with turquoises and an embroidered saddle-cloth elaborately worked. In this order the procession entered the city and the Pasha was taken to the residence designated for him. [Spencer, 1976]

It's interesting that Père Dan mentions the terror roused in "our" European hearts by the music. The Janissaries appear to have been the very first in history to use military marching music, and when their bands appeared blaring and booming before the gates of Vienna, it's said that Christian soldiers threw down their weapons and fled at the mere sound. It would be interesting to know if the *Ocak* ever shipped a band aboard a corsair vessel (the Algerian Janissaries accompanied the pirates as men-at-arms, used only when a prize ship was boarded and subdued by force). The European pirates who operated in the Caribbean and Indian oceans in the 17–18th century are reputed to have been very fond of music, and to have hired on full-time professionals when they could afford to, but apparently the music was for their own pleasure rather than a form of psychological warfare![8]

8. Spencer has this note on the various kinds of music to be heard in Algiers:

Algerian music was primarily military in nature, reflecting its Ottoman origins. The ocak military band consisted of twenty-seven pieces: eight large drums called davul, played with the fingers; five kettledrums (nakkare); ten bugles; two trumpets; and two pairs of cymbals. The type of music was mehter, a strongly accented rhythmic style popularized in the Ottoman Empire by the Janissary corps and synonymous with Ottoman

In Salé the Sufi and military Turkish music would have been unknown, but Andalusian music—a complex of Persian, Arab, Moorish, Iberian, and other influences, developed over centuries in Islamic Spain and now suddenly exiled to North Africa—must have been imported to Salé by various waves of Moors and Moriscos from Spain; new Berber and African influences would have been added to the mix giving birth to classical North Moroccan music more-or-less as it's played today—and still called *Andalusi*.

Salé, by contrast with the other Barbary states, remained free of Ottoman control or even much influence. A close relation between Algerine and Saletine corsairs (discussed below) probably led to *some* Turkish cultural influence in Salé. For instance, Salé celebrated a special holiday with the old Turkish custom of a candlelight procession. But Salé was at all times either a Moroccan possession or a free Moorish-Corsair state, and no "foreigners" ever seized power there in the name of an alien government.

Structurally, the most notable feature of the Algerian *Ocak* was its system of "democracy by seniority." In theory—and for the most part even in practice—a recruit rose up through the ranks at the rate of one every three years. If he

---

military pomp and power. A second popular type of music was the Andalusian, brought by Morisco refugees from Spain and incorporating the use of such Oriental instruments as the 'oud, tar, rebeb (a two-stringed violin), and ney (a reed flute) featured in Anatolian Mevlevi dervish compositions, on a semitonal scale. During the period of the Regency, Andalusian orchestras of twenty or thirty persons could often be heard in Algerian cafés, "playing all by ear, and hastening to pass the time quickly from one measure to another, yet all the while with the greatest uniformity and exactness, during a whole night," as Renaudot tells us.

survived long enough, he'd serve as commander-in-chief or *"Agha of Two Moons"*…for two months. He would then retire into the Divan or *Ocak* chamber of government with a vote on all important issues and appointments. All this had nothing to do with "merit", but was simply a matter of *time served*. The lowliest Albanian slaveboy or peasant lad from the Anatolian outback, and the outcast converted European captive sailor, could equally hope one day to participate in government — simply by *staying alive* and serving the "Corsair republic", which was the real power-structure within the Ottoman protectorate. As Père Dan put it: "The state has only the name of a kingdom since, in effect, they have made it into a republic." No wonder the *Ocak* never seemed to have trouble recruiting new members. Where else in the world was such "upward mobility" possible?

The Divan itself used one of the strangest "rules of order" ever devised by any group anywhere in the world:

> The rules covering the meetings of the divan were simple enough. No member was allowed to carry arms of any kind, and armed guards maintained order. No member was allowed to use his fists for any offensive action on pain of death, but he was allowed to express his feelings with his feet, either by stomping or by kicking. One French consul was nearly killed when he was "footed" in the divan. All speech was in Turkish; dragomen translated into Berber or Arabic and the European languages when necessary. The "word" was taken in order of seniority or importance, although the most usual practice seems to have been for the speaker to orchestrate a chorus of shouting by the assembly. These sessions were incredibly

disorderly as a result of this procedure. Foreigners who attended were often convinced that they were dealing with wild, violent, irrational men; the evidence seems to point to the fact that the leaders used this procedure to emphasize their programs and to shout down any objections. To an Englishman, however, such procedures seemed irrational; for instance, Francis Knight, who, in the second quarter of the 17th century spent several years in Algiers as a slave, was apparently able to witness meetings of the divan. His account of procedures is worth repeating:

"They stand in ranks, passing the word by *chouse* or *pursuivant*, jetting each other with their arms or elbows, raising their voices as if in choler or as a pot boileth with the addition of fire…. They have a wise prevention of a greater mischief, for [they] are commanded upon deepest pains not to drink wine or any strong liquor before coming…or to carry a knife thither…. It is such a government like which there is nowhere else in the world…" [Wolfe, 1979: 78]

In the course of its long run for the money, Algiers witnessed every sort of skullduggery, riot, rebellion, corruption, political murder, and disorder known to the human condition—and yet somehow survived and thrived. Some have gone so far as to define its form of government as "democracy by assassination". But was it any more corrupt or violent than any other state in the 17th (or any other) century? Was it so much more chaotic than, say, the European monarchies, so wild that it could boast of a freedom obtained—at least for

the successful few—and obtainable only through chaos? Or do the accounts (by European visitors, remember) over-stress the negative and present us with a wicked caricature of Algiers? My suspicion is that the daily life of the City was no more or less violent over the long haul of history than the daily life of many another human group. But Algiers was different because its very economy depended on violence *outside* its borders—the acts of the corsairs. And it *was* more democratic than the European or Islamic monarchies. Are these two features somehow *connected*? I prefer to leave it a question.

The corsair equivalent of the Divan was the *Taiffe reisi*, or Council of Captains. Unfortunately we know a good deal less about it than about the Divan, because the corsairs had no Ottoman bureaucrats and *hocas* (learned scribes) to serve them as record-keepers. The Taiffe has been compared to a medieval guild, but this is misleading to the extent that the Corsairs' proto-labor-union was also a de facto ruling (or at least consultative) body within the Regency. The Divan and the Taiffe may sometimes have competed or clashed in power struggles, but we may be sure that neither body would lightly risk alienating the other. The Corsairs depended on the *Ocak* for political protection, funding, and a supply of men-at-arms. The Divan depended on the Taiffe for its economic life-blood, the very prosperity of the Regency, which lived, in large part, on pirate booty and ransom fees. Apparently the Divan of Salé was based on the structure of the taiffe of Algiers (rather than on the structure of the Divan of the *Ocak*), so it's a pity we know so little about Taiffe organization. Unlike the *Ocak*, seniority would obviously not work as a modus operandi. The reis was a captain either through sheer merit (or "luck" as most pirates would call it), or because he owned a ship or two. Of course, again, a lowly pirate cabin boy (like Hamida Reis) could hope to become Admiral of the Fleet some day, whatever his class or race ori-

gins—a far different situation than in, say, the British Navy! And we know that the Taiffe voted democratically on issues and to select its leaders. Altogether it may well be that the 16–17th century Algerian Divan-and-Taiffe form of "bicameralism" can be seen as a precursor to the republican governments of America and France, which came into being only *centuries later*; as for the genuine Republic of Salé, it preceded even the protectorate/Commonwealth structure of revolutionary England (1640's and 50's). A strange thought: Does European democracy actually owe a *direct debt* to the Corsairs? No one would ever have admitted it openly, of course, since the Barbary corsairs were *heathen*—but as Rediker points out, sailors were the 17th century's proletariat, and we might imagine whispers circulating from ship to ship (England sent a fleet to Salé in 1637!) about the enviable freedoms of the Corsairs and Renegadoes.[9]

---

9. In 1659, the Ottoman-appointed Pasha demanded a bigger cut of the Corsairs' booty:

> This produced a revolution that ended the powers of the pasha of Algiers. A boulouk-bachi, Khalil, rallied the divan to an insurrection to "re-establish the ancient ways." These "ancient ways" were alleged to be a constitution that placed all effective powers in the hands of the janissary agha and the divan. Of course, this was pure mythology, but like revolutionaries in mid-seventeenth-century England, France, Barcelona, Naples, and elsewhere, the Algerian divan insisted that it only wanted a return to ancient forms. No one in this era would admit to being a "revolutionary." The result, however, was revolutionary. A few years later d'Aranda could write, "The pasha…acknowledges a kind of subjection to the Grand Seigneur in words, but takes little account of his orders…. The soldiers are more dreadful to him than the Grand Seigneur." They had become the rulers of Algiers, leaving the pasha as a ceremonial officer, paid a regular salary, but without power. [Wolfe, 1979: 84]

IV

A COMPANY OF ROGUES

We must skip over the fascinating unfolding of political
structures in the subsequent history of Algiers, simply
because it cannot offer us much help in understanding our
chief interest, Salé. As for what we might call the specific
ethnography or socio-history of Algerian piracy, we will certainly return to it for comparative material when discussing,
say, the erotic mores or economic arrangements of the
Corsairs of Bou Regreg in Morocco. But one more Algerian
theme must detain us before we depart for the Far West —
the Renegadoes.

A huge proportion — some say the majority — of Algerian
captains and crews were indeed "foreigners" of some sort or
another. Andalusian Moors and Moriscos from Spain introduced new techniques in armory and cannon, and many of
them proved experienced mariners as well. A medley of
"Levantines" from the Eastern Mediterranean — including
Greeks, Egyptians, Syrians, islanders, and the usual riffraff
and scum of every port — served the *jihad* in Algiers.
Albanians and other Balkan/Ottoman mountaineers and
brigands floated in along with the Turkish contingent. And
of course there were Renegadoes from every country of
Europe (especially the Mediterranean littoral), whether volunteers or converted captives:

Between 1621 and 1627 there were said to be twenty thousand Christian captives in the corsair capital, including "Portuguese, Flemish, Scots, English, Danes, Irish, Hungarians, Slavs, Spanish, French, Italians; also Syrians, Egyptians, Japanese, Chinese, South Americans, Ethiopians," which attests to the polyglot ethnicity of seafaring in those days. The records kept by Redemptionists on apostasy are equally revealing, although painful to the apostolic ego. Between 1609 and 1619, Gramaye observed, renegades who willingly abjured their faith for the comforts of Islam included "857 Germans, 138 Hamburgmen, 300 English, 130 Dutch and Flemings, 160 Danes and Easterlings, 250 Poles, Hungarians and Muscovites."

[Spencer, 1976: 127]

Once a whole army of Spaniards embraced Islam to avoid captivity, and were apparently completely absorbed — and even a few Black Africans, brought north in slave caravans, who purchased their own freedom and joined the great corsair gold-rush. Jews, both native and foreign (including Marranos and Convertados from Spain, and other Sephardic groups), served all the Barbary states as merchants and financiers, and frequently obtained great power in the councils of government. European merchants, consuls, and redemptionist friars and priests provided a small shocked audience for this exotic rainbow coalition of rogues, and luckily some of them wrote up their impressions and memoirs. The pirates themselves have left us not a word.

The hero and beau ideal of the Corsairs was Khaireddin (Khizr) Barbarossa (Redbeard), the greatest scion of a fam-

ily of sea-rovers (probably Albanian in origin but resident on Lesbos), who first arrived in the Western Mediterranean as an agent of the declining Mameluke power of Egypt. From Tunis, he and his brothers joined with Moors from Granada to raid Spanish coasts. They raised their own freelance fleet and sold their services to various North African regimes; when possible they would assassinate the local ruler and take over the town (Bougie, 1512, Jijelli, 1514, Algiers, 1515); the island of Djerba for a time served as their headquarters. Around 1518, hard pressed by Spain, Khaireddin appealed for aid to the Ottoman Sultan Selim I (the "Grim"), and was appointed vice-regent or *beylerbey* of Algiers. He finally managed to expel the Spaniards from their island fortress in the bay of Algiers in 1529, and took Tunis in 1534.[10] The emperor appointed him admiral of the entire Turkish fleet. The Ottomans had a treaty with France at the time, and Barbarossa appeared off the coast of Provence as an ally. But so powerful was he that he prohibited the ringing of church bells (an offensive sound in Islamic tradition) while his fleet was anchored in port. He died in bed in his palace at Constantinople, and was succeeded as beylerbey of Algiers by his son Hassan Barbarossa. A true pirate epic, rags to riches: the Renegadoes' dream. [Spencer, 1976: 18]

In the next generation the Renegado hero was Morat Reis, another Albanian, who made a name for himself by capturing a Sicilian duke and plundering a papal galley.

---

10. When Khaireddin was about 50, he captured a young Italian noblewoman, Marie de Gaetano, and married her. Wolfe mentions also that the wife of one of the later Deys of Algiers was "an English renegade". Perhaps we can permit ourselves to imagine that not all such wives were unhappy captives, but that some of them enjoyed the adventure.

His most daring adventure, however, was to take a squadron of four galiots through the Straits to Salé, where he was joined by three pirate captains, and then on to the Canaries. The corsairs sacked Lanzarote, captured the wife and daughter of the governor and hundreds of people of lesser importance. After a cruise around the islands and several further landings for more booty and prisoners, they hoisted a flag for parley and allowed the ransom of their more important captives. The rest were carried back to Algiers or Salé as slaves. The Spanish, forewarned of the corsairs' return, tried to intercept them at the Straits, but Morat Reis successfully evaded Don Martin de Padilla's armada in a storm and brought his little flotilla into Algiers. It was a daring raid made more daring since the galiot was not really a suitable vessel for the Atlantic. Christians liked to believe that God punished Morat Reis by causing his son to die just before his return, but the story, told in the testimony about the raid made before the Inquisition, may not be completely correct. [Wolfe, 1979: 146–7]

Morat Reis seems to have inaugurated the special "Salé connection" in Algiers, which led to a unique scheme for the mutual benefit of both cities. When Algiers signed a peace-treaty with some European nation—a frequent occurrence in the complex web of diplomatic back-stabbing around the Mediterranean basin—then Algiers agreed not to raid the shipping of that country—say, England. Meanwhile, let's say, Salé is temporarily at peace with France, and thus French

ships are taboo for the "Sally Rovers". So…when an Algerian corsair approaches a French ship, it flies the flag of Salé, and thus arouses no suspicion. Having seized the French ship, it reverts to Algerian colors and returns to Algiers (where French prizes are permitted) to sell cargo and captives. And a ship from Salé can pull the same trick on a ship from England. Further ramifications can be imagined, especially as Algerian and Saletine ships could freely use each other's home port facilities for repairs, sale of booty, and R & R.

Ali Biçnin (a corruption of his name, Picenino) flourished in Algiers during the same period (1630's–60's) which also saw the establishment of the Bou Regreg Republic in Morocco, and which seems to have been the real golden age of the Barbary corsairs.

> He was an Italian, some say a Venetian, named Piccinio, who arrived in Algiers in command of a pirate ship that he had sailed from the Adriatic; he converted to Islam and quickly rose to prominence in the taiffe through his daring and bravery. His prizes made him rich, and he reinvested in new corsair vessels until his own flotilla earned him the title of admiral of Algiers. He owned two palaces in the city, a villa in the suburbs, several thousand slaves, jewels, plate, and great wealth in merchandise. He built a sumptuous public bath and a great mosque in Algiers as a gift to the city. He had his own bodyguard of footmen as well as cavalry, recruited mostly from the Koukou tribesmen whose sultan became his father-in-law. In the 1630's the redemptionist fathers writing from Algiers looked to him rather than the pasha as the real ruler of the city. Francis

43

Knight, who was one of his slaves, called him a great "tyrant" who respected no man, not even the Grand Seigneur. However, not all his slaves regarded their lot as "exquisitely miserable" or their master as a tyrant. One story tells of a Mohammedan fanatic who, wishing to gain paradise by killing a Christian, begged Bitchnin for the privilege of killing one of his slaves. The corsair agreed but armed a muscular young man with a sword and then invited his petitioner to meet him in an orchard; when he fled, Ali Bitchnin laughed derisively at him. Another slave returned a diamond that he had "found"; Bitchnin remarked about the folly of not taking advantage of a chance for freedom!

Ali Bitchnin probably had ambitions to usurp control over the regency. His alliance with the sultan of Koukou, his bodyguard of hundreds of soldiers, his personal navy, his relations with the coulougli leaders all point to political ambitions. He suffered a serious reverse at Valona, where he lost eight galleys (Knight secured his freedom from him in that battle; he was a slave on board of one of the ships that was captured) and two thousand slaves. A few years later, when the sultan planned an assault on Malta, Ali Bitchnin refused to allow the Algerian naval forces to go unless the sultan would pay a subsidy in advance. The Sublime Porte sent a *chaouch* (messenger or emissary) to Algiers to secure Ali Bitchnin's head; both the chaouch and the pasha had to flee to a mosque to escape the wrath of the corsair admiral's followers. At

that point, however, the pasha refused to pay the Janissaries' salary, and the corps demanded that Ali Bitchnin provide the money. Apparently, he had not yet prepared his men for a coup. He fled to his father-in-law's territory, and the Janissaries sacked his city homes as well as the Jewish quarter. What would happen next? The Sublime Porte obviously feared that Ali Bitchnin might return to Algiers with a Kabyle army; it sent him money, pardon, and honors just short of making him the pasha, but when he returned to Algiers with the sultan's chaouch, he soon sickened and died. His funeral was celebrated with near royal pomp, but many suspected that he had been poisoned on the sultan's orders.

[Wolfe, 1979: 148-9][11]

Simon Danser, the "Old Dancer" or "Diablo" Reis, was the famous corsair who (according to legend, at least) first taught the North Africans to abandon their outmoded Mediterranean rowed galleys with lateen rigs and take up sailing in "round ships", i.e., European-style fore-and-aft-rigged vessels (like the caravel, made famous by Columbus). Danser and his comrade Captain Ward (who will re-appear later) achieved enough fame to appear as characters in

---

11. Ali Biçnin's mosque, built in 1622, was based on Ottoman models, with "an octagonal cupola set on a central arcaded square courtyard, with smaller octagonal cupolas serving as the roofs of the arcades." [Spencer, 1976: 77] Building a mosque is no proof of a sincere conversion, of course, but it does demonstrate that Ali Biçnin at least wished to appear pious.

Thomas Dekker's play, *If This be not a Good Play, the Divel is in it* (1612) [Ewen, p. 3]. Originally a Dutchman from Dordrecht,

Danser came to Algiers from Marseilles, where he had established residence, married, and engaged in the ship-building trade. It is not clear what caused him to turn renegade and undertake a corsair career, but within three years of his arrival he had become the taiffe's leading reis and had acquired the sur-name of Deli-Reis, "Captain Devil," for his audacious exploits. Using captured prizes as models, Danser taught his fellow captains the management and navigation of round ships equipped with high decks, banks of sails, and cannon. He personally accounted for forty prizes, which were incorporated into the cor-sair fleet, and from Danser's time onward the Algerians replenished their losses equally from captured ships and from their own shipyard.

Danser also led the Algerians farther afield than they had ever navigated before. They passed through the Strait of Gibraltar, penetrated the Atlantic, and ranged as far north as Iceland, where a corsair squadron swept the coast in 1616....

Ironically, Danser, who seems to have retained his Christian faith at least in secret, utilized the capture of a Spanish ship carrying ten Jesuit priests off Valencia as a means of informing the French Court of Henri IV secretly of his intention to return to Marseilles, where he had left his wife and children. The

French agreed on condition of the safe return of the Jesuits, which was done. In 1609 Danser was reunited with his family and restored to full citizenship by the Marseilles city council. But, once a corsair always a corsair, whether in the service of Christian France or Muslim Algiers, and in 1610 Danser presented to the king and the Marseilles councilors a bold proposal for an expedition against Algiers which—given his extraordinary inside knowledge of the city—would probably have overthrown the Regency government. Unfortunately, the French, distrustful of the loyalty of the former corsair, refused to entertain his project. [Spencer, pp. 125–6]

The Old Dancer, however, was in fact the *causus belli* of a war between France and Algiers. It seems that

Danser, grateful for generous treatment by the French government, presented the Duc de Guise, the governor of the province, with two brass cannons, which, unfortunately for subsequent events, were on loan to him from the government of Algiers. Naturally the Algerians, shocked at Danser's "treason", demanded the return of the two cannons.

The political crisis moved slowly but surely. Guise refused to give up his cannons, but it was events in France, quite unconnected with Danser, that delayed action. Henry IV was murdered, the regent Marie de Medici had troubles to worry about both in the Rhineland and in Paris. Nothing was done. This was the

sort of crisis that the Algerian reis were waiting for: French Mediterranean commerce was
plentiful and rich and tempting, and with the
refusal of the French king to grant redress, it
was an excellent opportunity for the corsairs.
[Wolfe, 1979: 181-2]

The cannon were eventually returned to Algiers—perhaps the worst humiliation ever suffered by France at the
hands of its future colony.

We could go on digging up the names of many Algerian-
based Renegadoes, and even the names of some of their ships
and prizes, but we wouldn't learn very much more about
their lives, much less their thoughts and feelings. Needless to
say that some of them were Moslems, at best, in name only,
and were despised by the pious for continuing to drink,
curse, and "sing like Christians" even after their conversion.
But what about that sailor from St. Tropez who caused a
diplomatic incident because the French consul tried to prevent his turning Turke? What were *his* motives? And what
about Ali Biçnin's mosque and bath house? The architecture
of a cynical hypocrite?—or perhaps the sign of a more
ambiguous emotion, half self-interest, half something else?
True insincerity is—after all—rather rare in the history of
the human heart. Most people tend to justify their choices
and acts by some appeal to ideas and ideals—and first of all,
to justify these acts to *themselves*. Ideologies are easily inter-
nalized when self-interest and self-image coincide with ideological rhetoric and goals. To assume that the Renegadoes
were all Machiavellian schemers and poseurs would be to
give them too much credit. It's far more psychologically convincing to imagine that some of them, at least, came to
"believe" in what they professed to believe.

The ambiguity of the Renegadoes was mirrored even in language. The medley of peoples in Algiers must have produced a polyglot nightmare of mistranslation. A lingua franca was needed, and indeed came to be known as *Franco*, the language of the "Franks" (and by extension of all European foreigners), or *Sabir* (from the Spanish "to know"). Arabic, Spanish, Turkish, Italian, and Provençal were mixed in this typical seaport argot. If a parallel dialect developed in Salé, it might have utilized Arabic, Berber, Hispano-Arabic (Morisco) and Spanish, Portuguese, French, and English. "New" languages reflect new and unique large–scale social phenomena; they are not simply means of communication but also *patterns for thinking*, vehicles for the inner and outer experience of the speakers, for their new *communitas*, and their new (or newly-adopted) ideology. *Franco* died out with the corsairs, but its shadowy existence suggests that the Renegadoes had become—however tenuously—a "People", a linguistic community. Given the right historical circumstances, a lingua franca can become a full-fledged literary language, like Urdu or Bahasa Malay. *Franco* never made the grade—but knowing that it existed must change our view of the Renegadoes. We can no longer see them as a random scattering of lost apostates. A language (however crude and jury-rigged) is a culture, or at least the sure sign of an emerging culture.

PORTRAIT OF WILLIAM LITHGOW
FROM HIS *TOTALL DISCOURSE OF RARE ADVENTURES*

V

An Alabaster Palace in Tunisia

Before we set sail at last for Salé we should make one more brief cruise of the Mediterranean in search of Renegadoes. It's incredibly frustrating not to have a genuine *biography* of one of these men (or women). In most cases all that survives of their memory is an anecdote or two, perhaps an exciting account of a battle at sea, which all reveal precisely nothing of the renegades' psychology, their thoughts, their motivations. But every once in a while a little flash of sulphurous insight lights up the gloom of mere speculation. For instance, the English Renegado Peter Eston,

> who started life as a Somerset farm laborer, commanded a fleet of forty vessels by 1611. In 1612 he raided the fishing fleet on the Newfoundland banks, as West Indian-based pirates were to do after him. Here he trimmed and repaired his vessels, appropriated such provisions and munitions as he needed, and took 100 men to join his fleet. He caused havoc wherever he appeared, whether this was in the western Mediterranean or off the coast of Ireland. Eventually tiring of the renegade life,

he entered the service of the Duke of Savoy, purchased a Savoyard marquisate, and married a lady of noble birth. [Lucie-Smith, 1978: 83]

At one time, Eston was told that James I of England had offered him a pardon. "Why should I obey a king's orders," he asked, "when I am a kind of king myself?" This quip reminds us of numerous speeches recorded in Defoe's *General History of the Pyrates* which hint at the existence of a pirate "ideology" (if that's not too grand a term), a kind of proto-individualist-anarchist attitude, however unphilosophical, which seems to have inspired the more intelligent and class-conscious buccaneers and corsairs. Defoe relates that a pirate named Captain Bellamy made this speech to the captain of a merchant vessel he had taken as a prize. The captain of the merchant vessel had just declined an invitation to join the pirates:

> I am sorry they won't let you have your sloop again, for I scorn to do any one a mischief, when it is not to my advantage; damn the sloop, we must sink her, and she might be of use to you. Though you are a sneaking puppy, and so are all those who will submit to be governed by laws which rich men have made for their own security; for the cowardly whelps have not the courage otherwise to defend what they get by knavery; but damn ye altogether: damn them for a pack of crafty rascals, and you, who serve them, for a parcel of hen-hearted numbskulls. They vilify us, the scoundrels do, when there is only this difference, they rob the poor under the cover of law, forsooth, and we plunder the rich under the protection of our own courage. Had you not better make

them one of us, than sneak after these villians
for employment?

When the captain replied that his conscience would not
let him break the laws of God and man, the pirate Bellamy
continued:

> You are a devilish conscience rascal, I am a
> free prince, and I have as much authority to
> make war on the whole world as he who has a
> hundred sail of ships at sea, and an army of
> 100,000 men in the field; and this my con-
> science tells me: but there is no arguing with
> such snivelling puppies, who allow superiors
> to kick them about deck at pleasure.

It's interesting to compare Eston, a "farm laborer" with
the heart of a king, with Henry Mainwaring, the gentleman
pirate who *did* accept an English pardon and (like Henry
Morgan some years later) betrayed his former low companions. Or consider the only real aristocrat (as far as I know)
to turn Turk, Sir Francis Verney:

> A turbulent youth, Verney lost a quarrel with
> his stepmother about his inheritance, and in
> the autumn of 1608 left England in disgust. He
> arrived in Algiers and played a part in one of
> the frequent wars of succession, then turned
> corsair. In 1609 he was reported by the
> English ambassador in Spain to have taken
> "three or four Poole ships and one of
> Plymouth." In December 1610 he was said by
> the Venetian ambassador in Tunis to have
> apostasized. At this period he was an associate

of John Ward. But his period of success did
not last long. In 1615, according to Lithgow,
he was desperately sick in Messina, after being
a prisoner for two years in the Sicilian galleys.
He had been redeemed upon his reconversion
by an English Jesuit. Though he was now free,
his fortunes were broken, and he was forced to
enlist as a common soldier in order to exist.
Lithgow discovered him when he was on the
point of death, "in the extremist calamity of
extreme miseries" and having lost all desire to
live. [Lucie-Smith, 1978: 84]

Four years later (1615) he died in the Hospital of St.
Mary of Pity at Messina [Senior, 1976: 98]. Truly he "came
to a bad end", as the old-time chroniclers always said of the
pirates—whether it was true or not.

Another English renegado "gentleman" (from Cornwall)
was Ambrose Sayer [*ibid.*, p. 83]. In 1613 Sayer was captain
of an Algerian vessel which was captured at Salé by an
English ship, whose captain decided to send the corsairs
back to London to stand trial. Toby Glanville, one of Sayer's
shipmates, realized the "game was up, made several attempts
to commit suicide and eventually succeeded in throwing himself off the stern of the ship." [*ibid.*, p. 97] Presumably, like
most sailors, he'd never learned to swim. Captain Sayer was
sent home and convicted of piracy, but somehow managed to
escape—and presumably to retire, since we hear no more of
him.

Probably the corsair about whom we know the most was
John Ward. Ward enjoyed the distinction of "starring" as the
villain of that 1612 West End hit, *A Christian Turn'd Turke*;
Ward also merited at least two penny-dreadful blackletter
pamphlets and two popular ballads—the supermarket

tabloids of the good old days—which may be full of errors and outright lies, though they paint an interesting picture. [For Ward, see Ewen, 1939]

Ward was born around 1553, "a poore fisher's brat" in Faversham, Kent. In the last year of Elizabeth's reign and the first of James, we find him penniless in Plymouth, apparently with a fairly extensive career in privateering behind him—fifty years old, "squat, bald, white-haired." [Norris, 1990: 63] In 1603 he had the extreme bad luck to be "drummed into service" in the Navy—i.e., impressed—and forced to serve aboard the *Lion's Whelp* under Captain Thomas Sockwell (who later became a pirate himself). As many historians have noted, low or non-existent pay, exhausting drudgery, and violent corporal punishments made up life in the Navy in those days, which was "one of the worst fates that could befall any man."[12] Ward is said to have lamented his salad days in privateering "when we might sing, drab [i.e., fuck], swear and kill men as freely as your cakemakers do flies; when the whole sea was our empire where we robbed at will, and the world was our garden where we walked for sport." After just two weeks of naval discipline Ward reasserted himself and organized thirty other sailors to jump ship, steal a small bark in Plymouth harbor,[13] and sail out on the Account, free men at last. Aged 50, Ward embarked on a new and amazing career—as a pirate.

---

12. Senior, p. 87. Dr. Johnson remarks somewhere that any sensible person would prefer prison to the British Navy; one could be sure, at least, of better food and companions!

13. He'd been planning simply to rob the ship of its treasure, which belonged to an English Catholic recusant fleeing to Spain, but apparently he'd been misinformed and found "the goldfinches flowen out of their nest" — so he stole the ship instead.

Ward now sailed to southern Ireland, probably to Bearehaven or Baltimore, obscure and remote little ports known for their hospitality to pirates.[14]

Somewhere in the area he came across the *Violet* of London in November 1603 and captured her.

> When they reached the Scilly Isles the pirates had the good luck to fall in with a French vessel, but such was the strength of their ship that they could only hope to capture the Frenchmen by guile. Accordingly, the majority of the pirates hid below hatches while a few of their comrades up on deck engaged the other ship in conversation. They continued thus for several hours until their ruse finally succeeded and they came close enough to board and overpower their quarry.
>
> [Senior, p. 88]

14. Six years later, in 1609, Ward and his comrade Captain Bishop visited Munster again at least once. Local officials had to be imprisoned for dealing with the pirates, who, after all, had 10 or 11 ships and about 1,000 men. Unable to repel them by force the English "Vice-President" of Munster tried to pardon them instead — but this expedient also failed. Later that year the British Lord Admiral sent a ship to Barbary under one Captain Pepwell to persuade Ward and his confederates "to forsake their wicked course of life." His mission not only failed, but all his sailors deserted him and joined Ward. Pepwell had to "part with his pinnace at an under rate to the Turks" and return to London looking foolish. Captain Bishop, who now claimed to despise Ward for turning Turke (in 1609), was bribed to murder him, but failed. Bishop pleaded for a pardon, saying supinely: "I will die a poor labourer in mine own country, if I may, rather than be the richest pirate in the world." [Ewen, 1939: 20-21] Ward obviously had other plans.

Ward renamed the ship *Little John*—which offers us a precious insight into his ideas and his image of himself: clearly he considered himself a kind of Robin Hood of the seas. We have some evidence that he gave to the poor, and he was clearly determined to steal from the rich.[15]

Ward now made one last clandestine visit to Plymouth, where he recruited a crew to man his flagship, and then set out for the South—and the Orient—never to return.

On his voyage south, Ward took a 100-ton flyboat north of Lisbon and then entered the Straits. He sailed to Algiers, but received a hostile reception there because Richard Gifford, an English adventurer in the service of the Duke of Tuscany, had recently attempted to burn the galleys in the harbor. He therefore continued to cruise the Mediterranean, increasing in strength and wealth all the time. In December 1604 he was in the waters of Zante, where he captured the *Santa Maria,* a Venetian vessel laden with currants and silk, and on Christmas Day that year he looted a Flemish ship of her cargo of pepper, wax, and indigo.

Disposing of his loot in various Mediterranean ports, Ward then passed through the Straits once more to trim and victual his ship. It was while he was at Salé, on the Atlantic coast of Morocco, that he was joined by twenty-three more Englishmen. These men, who had set sail in the *Blessing* with Dutch letters of marque, were in a sorry state, having been roughly handled by a Spanish warship. When they saw that Ward and his fellows were "well shipped and full of monie,"

---

15. In or about 1604, Ward arrived in Salé "to victuall and tryme his shippe haveing sould all their goodes"; there he joined with other pirates to raise and "disburse £100 to redeem a countryman" from captivity [Ewen, 1939: 3]. Ward used his own money to ransom captives on several other known occasions; perhaps this was his method of "giving to the poor".

they needed little encouragement to leave their ship and join forces with them. Ward's numbers were further augmented at Larache, when another English crew threw in their lot with him. The captain of these men, Michael, soon returned home to England, but their lieutenant, Anthony Johnson, remained with Ward and became one of his most trusted men.

By 1605 Ward had succeeded in gathering a formidable force around himself. His man-of-war, which he had appropriately named the *Gift*, was a flyboat of 200 tons or more, mounting thirty-two guns and crewed by about 100 men. In addition to the *Gift*, he was accompanied in his marauding by any prizes which he thought might suit his purpose. His men were mainly English, but included a considerable number of Dutchmen. There was certainly no shortage of able seamen who were anxious to join his band. Ward's pamphleteer, Andrew Barker, had an even higher estimate of the pirates' abilities, saying that many of them were "worthy spirits, whose resolutions, if they had beene aimed to honourable actions, either at sea or shore…might have beene preferred and commended for service to the greatest Prince living."

In 1603, Ward had been a common seaman, living in poverty and serving in terrible conditions aboard one of the king's ships. At fifty years of age it must have seemed that his best years were over. Now less than two years later, he was a rich man, the commander of a fine, strong vessel, and the respected leader of a large band of desperate men.

Ward's piracies continued throughout the winter of 1605–6. In November 1605 he was in the waters off Cyprus where he robbed a ship from Messina of silk, velvet and damask to the tune of £5,500. At about this time he also took a French prize laden with spices, drugs, and cotton in the roadstead at Modone, and followed this in April 1606 by capturing a Flemish ship off Sardinia, carrying a cargo of

textiles. Such captures can only have served to emphasize the pirates' growing need for a secure base of operations where they could sell their booty and store their riches. By 1606 they had found such a haven with the Turks at Tunis. In August of that year, Ward was reported to be living in the city and to have helped some English seamen who were temporarily in difficulties.

Ward's protector at Tunis was Cara Osman, who, as head of the Janissaries, had exercised absolute control over the city since 1594. An agreement was reached between the two men whereby Osman had first refusal of all goods which the pirates brought back to Tunis. The goods were then stored in Tunisian warehouses and resold to Christian merchants at a considerable profit. Everything points to the fact that Ward and Osman enjoyed a good working relationship and they may have even become close friends, for the pirate called the Turk "brother". The suspicion is, however, that Osman got the best of the bargain. Yet the pirates were utterly dependent on Osman's friendship, for without it they would probably have been denied the use of Tunis as a base. Thomas Mitton, a man who had lived at Tunis for three years and been to sea with Ward, testified to this when he gave evidence in the admiralty court:

> ...the said Carosman is the onelie aider, asister and upholder of the saide Warde in his piracies and spoiles for that hee the saied Warde hathe noe other place to victualle in save onelie Tunis, and at Tunis hee coulde not victualle but by the meanes of Carosman whoe grauntethe him the saied Warde warrantes to take upp and buy victualles at Tunis and the Cuntrie theereaboutes. And the reason that moovethe the saied Carosman soe to doe is

beecause when Warde takethe anie prize
Carosman buyethe his goodes of him at his
owne price.

Ward's first voyage from his new-found base began in
October 1606. Cara Osman paid one quarter of the costs of
victualling the pirate ship, which was the *Gift*, Ward's old
man-of-war. The crew was entirely English, except for
twelve Turks put aboard by Osman, who paid for their own
keep. Ward did not have to wait long for his first prize. On 1
November, near Corone, he captured the *John Baptist*, 90
tons, a vessel belonging to some London merchants which
was employed in the local coasting trade. At this capture the
Gift had as consort a fifty-ton pinnace commanded by
Anthony Johnson, and it seems reasonable to assume that
the two ships had set out from Tunis together.

The next prize to fall to the pirates was a far richer vessel, the *Rubi*, a Venetian argosy of upwards of 300 tons,
which was returning from Alexandria with a cargo of spices
and 3,000 pieces of gold. The *Gift*, flying a Dutch flag, sighted the *Rubi* on 28 January 1607, forty miles off the coast of
the Morea, and Ward and his men, no doubt making full use
of the element of surprise, captured her by boarding "verie
suddeine, desperate and without feare." Ward followed this
success by taking another Venetian vessel, the *Carminati*,
which was homeward-bound after a voyage to Nauplion and
Athens. Well pleased with the way the voyage had gone,
Ward returned triumphantly to Tunis with his two Venetian
prizes under guard.

As in the early years of the century, it was the Venetians
who once again had to bear the brunt of English depreda-
tions. They were, however, yet to suffer their most sensational loss.

Ward fitted out his ships and put to sea again early in

1607. This time he was in the *Rubi*, his Venetian prize which he had converted to a man-of-war and manned with a crew of 140, mostly English. Once again Cara Osman had bought a quarter share in the venture by providing the pirates with guns, powder, match, and shot from the Turkish armoury. This time, however, there were no Turks on the expedition.

The event that shook the Republic of Venice, and so enriched the pirates, was the loss of the *Reniera e Soderina*, a 600-ton argosy. The great ship was taken as she lay becalmed near Cyprus by two pirate ships commanded by Ward, each said to be mounting forty guns and carrying at least 100 armed men. Amongst the fabulous cargo of the *Soderina* was indigo, silk, cinnamon and cotton worth at least L100,000 (one wildly exaggerated English report put her value at "two millions at the least"). It was not only the size of the financial loss which caused such a stir on the Rialto. The very manner of the *Soderina's* capture was a disgrace to the Republic of St. Mark. From one account of the battle, it is clear that the crew of the argosy were terrified by the ferocity of the pirates' attack and offered little or no resistance:

> The captain, after deciding on the advice of everybody to fight, divided up all his crew and passengers, and stationed some on the quarter-deck, others on the maindeck and poop, and thus they all seemed to be very gallant soldiers with weapons in their hands. The two ships that came to attack, even though two or three shots were fired at them, strove without further ado to lay themselves alongside, and on coming within range fired off twelve shots, six each, always aiming at the crew and the sails, without firing once into the water. Their plans, designed to terrify, succeeded excellently,

because two of those who were defending the quarterdeck were hit by one of their shots, and when they were wounded, indeed torn to pieces, all the rest fled, leaving all their weapons lying on the quarterdeck and all of them running to their own property, even while the two vessels were coming alongside. For all his efforts, the captain was not only quite unable to force the crew to return to the quarterdeck, he could not even make them emerge from below decks or from the forecastle. Indeed, the ship's carpenter and some others confronted him with weapons in their hands and told him that he should no longer command the ship.

As if this prize were not enough, Ward proceeded to take another Venetian vessel before finally returning to his base. On a June day in 1607, he and his men dropped anchor at La Goleta, the port of Tunis, with booty worth at least 400,000 crowns. Ward did not want to prejudice his chances of getting a good price by landing the loot, and

> made many offers to carry away the shipp and goods to some other porte, because the said Carosman would not come to his price, and to that ende the said Warde rode out of command of the castle, and kepte his sayles at the yards, untill they had concluded.

Eventually, Ward and Cara Osman agreed on a price of 70,000 crowns—little more than one-sixth of what the goods were actually worth.

Ward was now at the height of his success. An English

seaman who saw him at Tunis in 1608 has left us a description of the arch-pirate:

> Very short with little hair, and that quite white, bald in front; swarthy face and beard. Speaks little, and almost always swearing. Drunk from morn till night. Most prodigal and plucky. Sleeps a great deal, and often on board when in port. The habits of a thorough "salt". A fool and an idiot out of his trade.
> [Senior, 1976: 88-93]

Whatever his level of intelligence "out of his trade", Ward was now at the high point of success *in* the trade. He

> gathered round him a formidable group of pirates: Captain Sampson was appointed to the command of prizes, Richard Bishop of Yarmouth became Ward's first lieutenant and James Proctor of Southampton and John Smith of Plymouth his gunners. Though Danser still rivaled him in the western Mediterranean, Ward ruled the central seas. When asked if he would like to join the French as Danser had done, he replied, "I favor the French? I tell you if I should meet my own father at sea I would rob him and sell him when I had done." When a seaman called Richard Bromfield upbraided him for turning Turk and living in such a heathenish country, Ward merely called him "a Puritan knave and a Puritan rogue."
> Yet at this moment he opened negotiations for a royal pardon. One of his acquaintances

deposed that he was offered £200 "in Barbary Gold" to take to friends in England in order to impress the Lord Admiral. The Venetian ambassador said that he was offered 30,000 crowns. But even James I jibbed at accepting bribes from such a notorious pirate and went so far as to name Ward specifically in a proclamation of January, 1609, for the apprehension of pirates. Ward seems to have been much annoyed at the rejection of his suit: "Tell those flat caps who have been the reason I was banished that before I have done with them I will make them sue for *my* pardon."

[Lloyd, 1981: 50-51]

As one of Ward's biographers put it, in a ballad called "The Famous Sea Fight between Captain Ward and the Rainbow," "Go tell the king of England, go tell him this from me / If he reign king of all the land, I will reign king at sea."

On one occasion in 1607, the well-known diplomat Sir Anthony Sherley "wrote to Ward at Tunis to dissuade him from his mode of life and sinful enterprises." Ward was so incensed he granted freedom to a ship he'd just captured, on condition that the Captain find Sir Anthony and convey to him Ward's challenge to a duel. It's hard to reconcile Ward's reputation for slow-wittedness with such flamboyant gestures.

About Sept. last (1608) Ward, being in the Straits, met Fisher of Redriffe, bound for England, and gave him £100 to carry to his wife. Others of the company also sent money for wives and friends. Fisher abused his trust. On their next meeting Ward despoiled Fisher's ship, and being reviled, had Fisher ducked at

the yard arm, and killed. The other men to avoid the like fate joined the pirates.

Ward having stabbed one West, a master's mate, his men mutinied. In a great storm in the straits under Saracota, Longcastle and others called him to prayers, but he refused, saying that "he neither feared God nor the devil." [Ewen, 1939: 14. These quotes and anecdotes derive from one of the pamphlets about Ward, *Newwes from Sea*.]

Ward now seems to have decided to remain in Barbary and give up all hope of a peaceful retirement. He

fitted out the *Soderina* as his man-of-war and made preparations for his next voyage. She must have looked a fine ship indeed: 600 tons burden, mounting forty bronze pieces on the lower deck and twenty on the upper. He was at sea in her by December 1607, in command of an Anglo-Turkish crew of 400. However, the *Soderina* soon proved to be impractical as a warship. Her excessive armament weighed her down and her planks began to rot. As soon as Ward captured a prize he took command of her, leaving his cumbersome warship to her fate. The great vessel sank off Cerigo early in 1608 with the loss of almost all hands—250 Turks and 150 Englishmen.

Yet this was just the start of a series of disasters that lay in store for Ward in the winter of 1607–8. First, the prize of which he had taken command was lost at sea, and then a galleon, which he had captured and fitted out

at Navarino, was wrecked. Worse still, one of his leading captains, a Fleming named Jan Casten, was off Modone on 21 March 1608 with two men-of-war and a prize when he was surprised and defeated by the Venetian galleys. In this, one of their rare victories over the pirates, the Venetians killed 50 men, including Casten, and captured forty-four more.

Ward still continued to serve in expeditions from Tunis after these setbacks. He sailed with two Turkish captains to the Levant in 1609 and went on further expeditions in 1610, 1612, and 1618. He even appears to have had a hand in the capture of a Venetian vessel in 1622, when he must have been nearly seventy years old. However, he developed other interests and stayed ashore more in his later years. He had soon become well-integrated into Tunisian society. By 1609 he had "turned Turk", taking the name Issouf Reis, and he is known to have married another renegade, a woman from Palermo named Jessimina (despite the wife in England to whom he periodically sent money). [Senior, 1976: 93-4]

In 1616 the gossipy Scots traveler William Lithgow met Ward at Tunis:

"Here in Tunneis I met an English Captain, general Waird [such was Lithgow's Scottish pronunciation: Father Dan called him Edouart], once a great pirate and commander

at sea; who in despite of his denied acceptance in England, had turned Turk and built there a fair palace, beautified with rich marble and alabaster stones. With whom found domestics, some fifteen circumcised English renegades, whose lives and countenances were both alike, even as desperate as disdainful. Yet old Waird their master was placable and joined me safely with a passing land conduct to Algier; yea, and diverse times in my ten days staying there I dined and supped with him, but lay aboard in the French ship." His legendary fame lived on because Edward Coxere, a captive at Tunis a few years later, says that Ward always "had a Turkish habit on, he was to drink water and no wine, and wore little irons under his Turk's shoes like horseshoes." [Lloyd, 1981: 53]

As a popular ballad put it:

> At Tunis in Barbary
> Now he buildeth stately
> A gallant palace and a royal place.
> Decked with delights most trim,
> Fitter for a Prince than him
> The which at last will prove to his disgrace.
> [Norris, 1990: 94]

Contrary to the balladeer's pious hope, Ward's architectural fancy failed to end in disgrace.

Lithgow also tells us that in his old age Ward had become interested in the problem of incubating poultry eggs in camel dung. One imagines him pottering about the alabaster palace with pots of this odiferous mulch, accompanied by curious chickens. The inevitable "bad end" which all

pirates must suffer was provided by the plague, which paid one of its regular visits to North Africa in 1623. Aged about seventy, Ward died in bed and was buried at sea just as he'd always expected and hoped.

> Ward's contemporaries in England wasted a great deal of vitriolic language on him and other English renegades, whom they saw in an almost medieval light, as having forsaken Christianity to espouse Islam. Yet one cannot but sympathize with the pragmatism of the pirates against the dogmatism of their day. Certainly Ward waged war on Christian shipping, making no exception of English vessels, but stories that he would have robbed his own father if he met him at sea seem simply malicious. There was certainly another side to his nature. On at least two occasions he is known to have freed Englishmen who found themselves enslaved at Tunis, and Lithgow, who actually met the man, referred to him as "Generous Waird." [Senior, p. 94]

C.M. Senior, the author of this epitaph, obviously cannot help a feeling of sympathy for Ward, despite his cruelty, bungling, and apostasy. The would-be Little John, the rather dimwitted old salt who no doubt continued to ramble on about the good old days over the dinner table,[16] makes an odd fit with the Tunisian gentleman, sometimes abstemious,

---

16. Once in 1608, Ward sailed into Algiers with a Spanish prize laden with a cargo of "alligant wines", and there met another pirate (one John King of Limehouse) who'd just captured a ship carrying beer. Ward traded him a tun of wine for a tun of beer, losing money on the deal, and revealing his working-class taste! [Ewen, 1939: 9]

"generous", and—who knows?—perhaps even a little pious. (It's interesting to note that Ward only converted rather late in his Tunisian career, which suggests he may have done so entirely voluntarily and even sincerely.) This almost adds up to a convincing character study; it has almost enough contradictions and paradoxes in it to sound psychologically authentic. No other Renegado comes across the gulf of time as such a fully-realized personality—with the possible exception of Murad Reis of Salé, whom we'll meet later on. Indeed, one can't help liking Ward—although, like William Lithgow, one might hesitate to spend a night at his alabaster palace, for fear of missing one's watch and wallet in the morning!

HORUSCE en HAREADEN BARBAROSSA

21
28
30 — "anarchalysts —
33-34 - music & terror
37 - Democracy & violence outside borders/Piracy
38 - bicameral govt Related?

92 — History is hard, Pirates dont write
Europeans do. → sensational fear

103 - Pardons

PIRATE UTOPIAS

MOORISH CORSAIRS &
Disloyalty EUROPEAN RENEGADOES

113-114 Pirate purchases

137 — Patriot vs Pirate

"Pirate Harbours" - Book

TABLE OF CONTENTS

ACKNOWLEDGEMENTS

The author wishes to thank the New York Public Library, which at some time somehow acquired a huge pirate-lit collection; the Libertarian Book Club's Anarchist Forums, and the New York Open Center, where early versions were audience-tested; the late Larry Law, for his little pamphlet on Captain Mission; Miss Twomey of the Cork Historical Society Library, for Irish material; Jim Koehnline for art, as always; Jim Fleming, ditto; Megan Raddant and Ben Meyers, for their limitless capacity for toil; and the Wilson Family Trust, thanks to which I am "independently poor" and free to pursue such fancies.

DEDICATION:

For Bob Quinn & Gordon Campbell, Irish Atlanteans

ISBN 1-57027-158-5

Autonomedia
PO Box 568, Williamsburgh Station
Brooklyn, NY 11211-0568
Phone & Fax (718) 963-2603
info@autonomedia.org   www.autonomedia.org
Printed in the U.S.A.

Pirate Utopias

Moorish Corsairs &
European Renegadoes

Peter Lamborn Wilson

Autonomedia

VI

THE MOORISH REPUBLIC OF SALÉ

The area around Salé appears to have been inhabited long before the emergence of *homo sapiens sapiens*. The Chalcolithic or "Pebble Culture" is well represented, and the Neanderthals were there. All levels of the Paleolithic are accounted for, and of course the Neolithic or "Atlantic Megalithic" [Brown, 1971]. The name Salé (Sala or Sla) may be exceedingly ancient, from the Berber word *asla*, meaning "rock". The old necropolis of Salé, called Chellah (really the same name again), dates back at least to Carthaginian times (around 7th century BC). The Romans called the place Sala Colonia, part of their province of Mauritania Tingitane. Pliny the Elder mentions it (as a desert town infested with elephants!). The Vandals vandalized the area in the 5th century AD, and left behind a number of blonde, blue-eyed Berbers. The Arabs (7th century) kept the old name and believed it derived from Sala, son of Ham, son of Noah; they said that Salé was the first city ever built by Berbers.

Salé was apparently somewhat tardy in converting to Islam, and became known to Moslems as a "frontier town"; but by the 9th century it was certainly Islamic, and the frontier had become the ocean itself. In the 10th century, when the Ismaili Fatimid Caliphate of Cairo conquered the Far

West, Salé apparently served as a military garrison: a fortress or *ribat*, built on the South bank of the Bou Regreg river across from Salé, became the settlement later known as Rabat. The military operations were directed against local Berber tribes who had adopted Kharijite doctrine (a kind of fundamentalism equally opposed to both Shiism and Sunni orthodoxy). By the 11th century, Salé had become an established city with essentially the same major features it still possesses. In order to understand subsequent events it's important to visualize the geographical and urban topography, hence this schematic diagram:

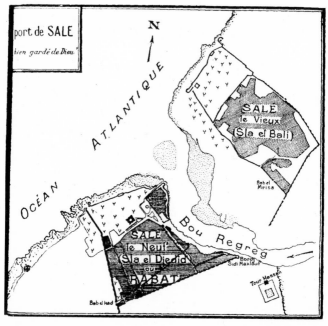

European commentators would later use the name Salé (Sallee or Sally) to refer to this entire complex, but in fact there are three distinct "cities" here, each of which will develop a separate and unique identity and fate: one, "Old" Salé (the present-day city of Salé). Two, the "Casbah" on the south side of the river, a little walled enclave unto itself. And three, "New" Salé (the basis for what would eventually be known as Rabat, the present-day capital of Morocco). In order to simplify matters we'll refer to these three settlements as *Salé*, the *Casbah*, and *Rabat*.

In the 11th century the first Spanish Moslems or "Andalusians" arrived in Salé from Cordoba, and brought with them their powerful and exquisite Moorish culture, architecture, music, spirituality, food, folkways, etc. At this point Salé took on its permanent sociological appearance—a port city where urban "Arab" Andalusian and rural Berber culture met, mingled, and mutated into *Moroccan* culture.

Under the Almoravids (1061–1164) and Almohads (1130–1269), Salé developed into an important nexus between trade with Europe and trade with Africa (the famous annual gold caravans), and became as well one of the recognized centers of Moorish culture, learning, piety, and sophistication. More Andalusians arrived, especially from Granada. Salé was already known as a place of refuge for the pious, a city of saints, marabouts, tombs, and shrines. Some of these saints will play an active role in our history—even (or perhaps especially) after their deaths. Two types of spirituality are represented here, comparable to the "urban" Andalusian and "rural" Berber elements in the cultural mix. That is, some saints were orthodox, intensely pious, involved in the classical literate Sufism of the Shadhili Order;[17] and

---

17. Originally from Egypt, founded by Abul Hasan al-Shadhili in the 13th century, divided into numerous branches all over the Islamic world, but especially Egypt, North Africa and Yemen. See Douglas (1993); az-Zirr and Durkee (1991).

others were more "maraboutic", i.e., heterodox, folkish, miracle-working. Many of the important saints of Salé appeared around the 13th century during the "golden age" of the Marinid dynasty (1216–1645), when rich trade with Europe and relative peace and prosperity in the Maghrib and Spain led to a great flowering of culture and architecture. Salé's famous mosque and Madrasa (theological school), still considered among Morocco's most beautiful buildings, were built under the Marinids, as were a hospital, an aqueduct, a hospice for Sufis, and other public works.

An exiled Vizier from Granada, Lisan al-Din (the "Tongue of the Faith") Ibn Khatib, visited Salé in the mid-14th century and raved about its beauty, and the delights of its bazaars, including "the most delicate of Abyssinian slaves"; perhaps he was thinking of them when he wrote a verse that became Salé's unofficial motto:

> Even distraction couldn't dispel
> grief from my heart
> but penetrated by the breeze of Salé
> it was salved.[18]

Around the same time one of Salé's most important saints—of the learned and orthodox variety—settled in the city: Sidi Ahmad Ibn Ashir, "the doctor", teacher of such famous Sufis as Ibn Abbad of Ronda, and also of a more maraboutic figure, a coral fisherman from Turkey known simply as "the Turk", who became a sort of patron-saint of local sailors. Sidi Ahmad Ibn Ashir himself could bless the ocean and quiet storms, so that his tomb later became a popular pilgrimage for pirates.

---

18. With a pun on Sala, the name of the city, and sala, Arabic for "console". See Brown, 1971: 34.

After the death of Ibn Ashir in 1362, Salé and the Marinids began a long slow slide into decay—but it was a peaceful and still fairly prosperous decadence. Leo Africanus, who visited the city in the 16th century, left this description:

> The houses are built in the style of the Ancients, much decorated with mosaics and marble columns. Moreover, all of the houses of worship are very beautiful and finely embellished. The same is true of the shops which are situated beneath large and beautiful arcades. In passing before some shops, one sees arches which have been built, it is said, to separate one craft from another.
>
> I have come to the conclusion that Salé possesses all of the luxuries which distinguish a city of refined civilization, as well as being a good port frequented by Christian merchants of various nationalities…. For it serves as the port of the Kingdom of Fez.
>
> Although Salé was quickly retaken [from the Castillan attack of 1260], it has since remained less populated and cared for. There are, especially near the ramparts, many empty houses with very beautiful columns and windows of marble and various colors. But the people of today do not appreciate them.
>
> The gardens are numerous, as well as the plantations from which a large quantity of cotton is gathered. Most of the inhabitants of the city are weavers and they also make a considerable number of combs at Salé which are sent to be sold in all of the cities of the Kingdom of Fez;

near the city is a forest full of Boxtree and other
kinds of wood that are good for making these.

In any case, people live very comfortably
today in Salé. There is a governor, a judge, and
numerous other officials — those of the customs
and the salt marshes — for many Genoese merchants come there and carry out important
affairs. Their trade creates important revenues
for the King. [quoted in Brown, 1971: 40–1]

The same period (late 15th–early 16th century) saw the
emergence of Salé's official patron saint, Sidi Abdullah Ibn
Hassun, who was — in a spiritual sense at least — deeply
involved in the unfolding of Salé's subsequent and unique
history. Sidi Abdullah represented an interesting mix of the
learned and the maraboutic traditions. He was neither especially learned nor descended from the Prophet,[19] but made
his living writing talismans. On his entry into Salé he was
followed by a walking palmtree which rooted itself on the
site of his future mausoleum. The Sufis of the city were so
ecstatic they changed into birds. And when the women of the
city came to visit him he turned himself into a woman so he
could receive them without scandal! The festival still held in
his honor is celebrated on the eve of the Prophet's birthday

---

19. Sayyids or Sharifs — descendents of the Prophet — are of course
honored everywhere in the Islamic world, especially by Shiites and
Ismailis, but they've played a major role in Sunni Morocco as well.
Great political prestige attaches to these families — one of them still
rules Morocco today. This veneration of the Sharifs may owe something to Fatimid influence, which still survives in popular lore in the
form of the famous "Hand of Fatima", used everywhere in North
Africa as a charm against the Evil Eye. See Westermarck (1968)
[1926]; see index under "Evil Eye", "Hand", etc.

(*Mawlid*), and is centered around a candlelight procession (based on Turkish custom) which the corsairs particularly enjoyed; they marched dressed in all their most colorful finery. Sidi Abdullah's most famous disciple was a marabout and holy warrior named Muhammad al-Ayyashi, who played a major role in the great era of the corsairs—which was now about to begin.

During the 15th and 16th centuries there was a dramatic change in the balance of power among the countries of the western Mediterranean. The fall of Muslim Granada in 1492 marked the end of over seven centuries of Moroccan expansion into and settlement in the Iberian Peninsula. Within a quarter of a century, all but one of the important maritime cities of the Moroccan Atlantic coast had fallen to the rising empires of Spain and Portugal. The exception was Salé.

Among the many people who came to Salé during this period was Mahammad al-Ayyashi (mentioned above as a disciple of Ibn Hassun) one of the most popular heroes of Moroccan history. Al-Ayyashi originated from the Banu Malik, one of the Hilali Arab tribes that had settled in the Gharb, the hinterland beyond Salé. Taking up residence in the city around the end of the 16th century, he is said to have devoted himself to a life of study and asceticism under the guidance of his shaykh Abd Allah b. Hassun and to have distinguished himself by piety, silence, continual fasting, and

reading of the Quran. One day, according to
the legend, Sidi Abd Allah was presented with
a horse by a group of tribal leaders who had
come to visit him. He called for his disciple al-
Ayyashi and told him to mount the horse and
to forego his education in order to discover,
with the help of God, his well-being in this
world and the one to come. The saint swore his
disciple by an oath to carry out his duty,
blessed him, and instructed him to ride to the
city of Azemmour.

Within several years of this legendary
episode, al-Ayyashi had become governor of
Azemmour, defender of southern Morocco
against the Spanish and the Portuguese, and a
dangerous rival to the Saadian dynasty that
had come to power during the first half of the
16th century. In 1614 al-Ayyashi narrowly
escaped an assassination planned by the
Saadian sultan and returned to Salé. From
then until his death in 1641 at the hands of an
Arab tribe of the Gharb, al-Ayyashi fought the
Spanish and Portuguese along the Atlantic and
the Mediteranean and became independent
ruler of the area north and east of Salé.
[*Hesperis*, 45]

The people of Salé had always welcomed Moors from
Spain into their community, both before and after 1492. In
the first decade of the 17th century, a new type of immigrant
began to appear. The last Moors of Spain, whether hold-
overs still adhering to Islam (*Mudejares*), or "*Moriscos*" (called
"Andalusians" in Salé) nominally converted to Christianity,
had been goaded by the racist and revanchist policies of

Spain into a series of revolts and had been expelled en masse by Philip II in a series of edicts between 1609 and 1614. One of Salé's traditional historians [*Hesperis*, 47] tells us that when these new refugees showed up and tried to rent houses there, "because of their non-Muslim ways, Spanish dress, language, and manners, their lack of shame and dignity, they were not allowed" to stay.[20] In 1610 a group called the Hornacheros (from Hornachos in Estremadura) arrived together as a cohesive people, still fervent Moslems and speaking Arabic, and quite wealthy. Unfortunately it seems that their wealth had derived from bribing Christian officials to let them carry arms, from brigandage and from counterfeiting; the Hornacheros were not deemed sufficiently *comme il faut* to settle in Old Salé, city of saints and shrines. So they moved south across the river and built up the Casbah, and settled there instead.[21]

The newly-arrived Moriscos however were even more outlandish—they spoke Hispano-Arabic or even Spanish, had Christian names and no wealth at all, and seemed even more vulgar than the Hornacheros. So the Moriscos had to content themselves with land below the Casbah (part of present-day Rabat), where they constituted a wholly separate group unto themselves. They thirsted for revenge against Spain and quickly became enthusiastic corsairs.

---

20. The newcomers had alien-sounding names like Vargas, Pelafres, Blanco, Rodriquez, Carasco, Santiago, Galan, Guzman, etc—and many of them knew not a word of Arabic. [Caillé, 1949: 248]

21. The Casbah included the ruin of the old ribat or fort. Abun Nasr calls it an Almohad construction; it was built (or re-built) around 1150, along with the tower of Hassan, a minaret which served as a landmark for vessels at sea. [Coindreau, p. 30–31]

All three cities of the Bou Regreg were now inhabited—just at the point when the Marinids had finally collapsed altogether, letting the whole of Morocco slide into a state of turmoil, civil war, and dynastic jockeying.[22] Nominal rulers of the land were now the Saadians of Marrakesh, far to the South, and not very well-organized.

Meanwhile, the Marabout al-Ayyashi had been gaining a name for himself in the *jihad* against Spain and other Christian powers encroaching upon Morocco—in fact, he is remembered to this day as a great hero of Moroccan nationalism. He had been set upon the path of holy war by his master Sidi Abdullah ibn Hassun, and had managed to make himself governor of Azemmour; he was highly unpopular both with the Europeans and with the Saadians of Marrakesh—who tried to have him assassinated in 1614, then sent an army against him.

He retreated back to Salé, where the leaders of all three cities agreed to protect him. Soon after (the date is uncertain), the Moriscos of Rabat declared themselves an independent republic, with a governor or "Grand Admiral" elected only for a very short term—a year at a time—and a divan or council of fourteen elders or advisors or captains. The Casbah followed suit in or around 1627 and created a Hornachero Republic. Both republics at first agreed to recognize al-Ayyashi's authority as "Commander in the Jihad" provided he respect their autonomy—but these good relations were not to last long.

Al-Ayyashi took up residence in Old Salé and built himself two forts just outside the city walls facing Rabat, with an underground tunnel (still extant) leading to his palace just

---

22. As one Moroccan historian put it, the universal turmoil was "enough to whiten the hair of a suckling babe!" See Caillé (1949: 209), quoting El-Oufrani.

inside the walls. The autocrats of the old city were his most enthusiastic supporters, and Salé now also declared itself independent under his spiritual/political authority. There were now three republics on the Bou Regreg—all engaged in Holy War—and piracy—and rebellion against the Saadians—and incessant quarrels with each other.

Around 1614, when the coastal city of Mamora fell to the Spaniards, a large number of international pirates fled to Salé and were welcomed by the Hornacheros and Andalusians.[23] They formed the nucleus of the Renegado community, and settled in Rabat—so actually the "Sallee Rovers" were Rabat rovers, although both settlements were commonly called Salé, and all three republics were involved in the corsair trade. Perhaps one might think of them as resembling three clans of Scottish Border Raiders, feuding incessantly with each other but teaming up for razzias on England. Sniping, quarreling, dissention, slurs on honor and other pastimes gave way to open civil war from time to time, especially between 1627 and 1641, but nothing was allowed to get in the way of business or impede the flow of booty.

This is a confusing situation, and the sources are also confused, but as far as I understand it, the situation was this: the Hornacheros financed piracy and built the fleet, and tended both to resent the old autocrats of Salé and to bully the lower–class Moriscos or Andalusians of Rabat. The

---

23. In effect, Mamora had functioned as a pirate republic under the inspired leadership of Captain Henry Mainwaring. This Englishman apparently never converted to Islam, which suggests that turning Turke was still a voluntary act, and one which he chose not to perform, despite his strong connection with Barbary. He later crowned a hugely successful career by "taking the pardon" and retiring to England, where he wrote an important treatise on navigation and lived like a gentleman. He also wrote a treatise on how to suppress piracy — don't offer any pardons, Mainwaring advised.

Andalusians served as men-at-arms on corsair vessels, and sometimes as spies (since they could pass as Spaniards). In their city of Rabat lived the international corsair community and the European merchants and consuls (on the rue des Consuls, still extant), and presumably this is where most of the taverns and whorehouses were to be found as well.[24] The Andalusians were the least enthusiastic of all three groups about al-Ayyashi and the Holy War, despite their original acceptance of him on the basis of a shared hatred of Spain. They resented his authoritarianism, and probably his attempts to interfere in their republican politics. Finally in exasperation they refused to help him with any further crusades—whereupon he turned his holy wrath upon them, and opened fire on Rabat with his precious cannon (both iron and the far-superior bronze variety), mounted on the walls of his forts in Salé.

Old Salé concerned itself primarily with al-Ayyashi's *jihad* and the rebellion against the Saadians—but the Slawis were certainly not above involvement in corsair activity, whether as investors, captains, crews, men-at-arms, or merchants of booty, captives, and slaves. Nevertheless, it's ironic that Salé is remembered as *the* corsair city, when that romantic title belongs so much more aptly to the Casbah/Rabat settlements across the river. To this day a rivalry between Salé and Rabat persists. As K. Brown puts it,

---

24. As Père Dan describes it, day and night the noise of quarrels arose from the taverns and Moorish cafés, most of them owned by indigenous merchants "to whom the pirates sold their booty"; the corsairs at once spent their profits in "cabarets and other places of debauch, since their greatest passion was to waste on revelry the wealth they'd won at sea." [Coindreau, 1948: 41] Some feeling for the "scene" might be gained from descriptions of Port Royal, the later pirate town in Jamaica, which was so wicked that a flood swallowed it up like a watery Sodom. [Exquemelin, 1699]

The struggles of the 17th century became in time vague historical memories. The Slawis, who had considered the new intruders at Rabat as *an-Naṣara 'l-Qaṣhtaliyin* (the Christians of Castille), came to call them *l-Mṣlmin ∂-r-Rbat* (coll., the Muslims of Rabat), a slightly humorous, partly bitter allusion to their laxity in religious matters. The Rabatis, with a comparable irony, remember the madness of the people of Salé. They say about them: *kayihmaqu fi-l-aṣr* (coll.: They go mad at the time of the afternoon prayer). The Slawis remember, too. They say that in the days of al-Ayyashi, while the people of Rabat treated with the infidels during the day, the Slawis went about their work. At the time of the evening prayer, however, they took up arms to fight against the traitors of Rabat. But the two cities within a sackershott one of another (following Admiral Rainsborough's phrase), became friendly enemies. They are called *al-a∂uwatayn* (the Two Banks) which, by the play of the Arabic root, reminds people of *al-a∂uwayn* (the Two Enemies). The mutual antipathy of the two populations becomes no more than bantering, and is expressed by both of them in a sagacious colloquial proverb: *wakha ywelli l-we∂ hlib war-rmel zbib, maykunṣhi r-Rbati li-ṣ-Slawi hbib* (Were the river [Bou Regreg] to become milk and the sand raisins, a Rabati will never be a friend to a Slawi). The friendly enemies across the river at Rabat were at the worst hostile brothers. For all that, they were Muslims and had assimilated to the

Arabic culture of the country.
[Brown, 1971: 50-51]

The initial quarrel between the Andalusians of Rabat and the Hornacheros of the Casbah centered on customs revenue, which the Hornacheros refused to share, saying they needed it all for defense and repair of the ramparts. The Andalusians remained unconvinced by these arguments, and by 1630 "the proud hosts of the Casbah and the disinherited inhabitants of the lower city were openly in a state of civil war." [Coindreau, 1948: 44] Old Salé sided with the Hornacheros, and ironically peace was restored only through the diplomatic intervention of the British consul, John Harrison,[25] who in May 1630 drew up an agreement which ended hostilities. The three points of the agreement were:

1st, the Andalusians would elect their own governor or *Caïd*, but he would reside in the Casbah;[26]

2nd, the Divan would comprise 16 notables each from the Casbah and new Salé;

3rd, revenues (including both maritime prizes and customs duties) would be equally divided between the Casbah and New Salé.

---

25. Harrison must have been popular. Charles I had signed a treaty with Morocco, and this "gentleman of the chamber of the Prince of Wales" had arrived with gifts for Salé, including six cannon. For Harrison's story, see pp. 105ff below. [Coindreau, 1948: 108.]

26. At this time the Hornacheros were led by Mohammed ibn Abd al-Qadir Ceron, and the Andalusians chose as Caid one Abdallah ibn Ali el-Caceri; both of them remained active in one office or another during the Republican period [Caillé, 1949: 217] — although Caceri was assassinated in 1638.

The two towns thus remained independent of each other and of Old Salé, but "in effect the Casbah became the central seat of the Moorish republic of Salé, and its government came to exercise a more-or-less preponderant authority over the cities of the two banks [of the Bou Regreg]." [Coindreau, 1948: 44]

The new balance of power proved precarious, and in 1631 al-Ayyashi broke the peace again. The Andalusians had betrayed him by refusing to send him the scaling ladders he needed in his seige of Mamora. He asked the religious leaders of Old Salé for a *fatwa* or decision allowing him to repress the corsairs of New Salé and the Casbah, "for they have opposed Allah and his Prophet and aided the infidels and given them counsel...they manage to their liking the property of Muslims, depriving them of profit and monopolizing trade to their benefit." [Brown, 1971: 49] Al-Ayyashi opened fire with his cannons and launched a seige against the South bank which lasted till 1632 and then fizzled out in October of that year.

Peace prevailed only a brief while, and in 1636 the Andalusians launched an attack against the Casbah which succeeded. Many Hornacheros fled the city, leaving the Moriscos in complete control. The victorious Andalusians now turned their wrath against Old Salé. They built a pontoon bridge over the Bou Regreg and initiated a siege of the city on the North bank. Al-Ayyashi, absent on the *jihad*, hurried back to defend his people.

Unfortunately for the Andalusians, the balance of power (which seemed to favor them) was now upset by the return of the English fleet, which had visited Salé the year before (under Lord Carteret, founder of New Jersey) to ransom English captives, and now re-appeared, on April 3, 1637, under the command of Admiral Rainsborough. An interesting account of this expedition has been left to us by a former pirate serving under Rainsborough.[27]

The English decided to treat only with al-Ayyashi, whom they called (no doubt with typical British irony) "the Saint". Perhaps the Marabout had refused to release English captives unless he received some help, but Rainsborough entered the fray with apparent enthusiasm, transferring some of his powerful up-to-date cannon from ship to shore, and beginning a bombardment of New Salé. The pontoons were sunk and the siege lifted. Al-Ayyashi, with British aid, effectively cut off all supply routes into the Casbah/Rabat area, and burned the fields outside the city walls.

Rainsborough weighed anchor on August 30, 1637, but the Andalusians had had enough. They capitulated, agreed to repair the damage done to Old Salé, allow the Hornacheros to return, and go back to the 50/50 split of duties and booty.

At this point the Saadian Sultan of Morocco decided to get back in the act; he hired one of the Renegado captains, a Frenchman named Morat Reis (not to be confused with the Albanian/Algerian captain of that name mentioned above, nor with the Dutch Renegado Murad Reis, whom we'll meet later) to capture the Casbah in the Sultan's name. Now the Andalusians and the Hornacheros patched up their animosity and joined arms to expel the Sultan's men, who had re-imposed the hated 10% tax, and in this effort they succeeded. But again the peace proved short-lived; within months al-Ayyashi had again decided to try wiping out the *"gens sans foi ni loi"* of Rabat. This time, the embattled Moors and Corsairs decided they needed an ally. Al-Ayyashi was a Sufi, so they

---

27. See Dunton, 1637; Carteret, 1638, published from MS in Philadelphia, 1929. Carteret himself later summed up his impression of Salé: "…[as] for the government, fundamentall lawes they have not any, for all that I could learne"! [*Sources Inédites* III, 1935: 453]

looked for help to a rival Sufi—one Mohammed al-Hajj ibn Abu Bakr al-Dala'i.

Muhammad al-Hajj's grandfather had been a great saint of the Middle Atlas region, where he established an important Sufi center and converted the local Berber tribes into a huge confraternity—the Dala'iyya. He taught the Jazuli/ Shadhili way of Sufism, centered on veneration of the Prophet, and an extensive program of public works and charity. Basically apolitical, the grandfather was succeeded by a son, who kept up cordial relations both with al-Ayyashi *and* with the Saadian Sultans (surely a proof of his diplomacy, if not his sanctity!)—but *his* son M. al-Hajj had political ambitions which began to sour the family's reputation for neutrality. Eventually M. al-Hajj succeeded his father as third head of the Order (1636) and began reorganizing it— as an army. [For this account, see Nasr, pp. 216–221]

In 1638 the Saadian Sultan sent his own army from Marrakesh to the Middle Atlas in an attempt to curb al-Hajj's growing ambitions, but the Saadians were completely routed by al-Hajj's Berber troops and fled South again leaving him in control of the whole area. He now decided his new *royaume* needed a seaport, and turned his holy gaze on Salé. Coincidentally just at that moment came the desperate appeal of the Andalusians, once again beseiged in Rabat by "the Saint" al-Ayyashi.

Muhammad al-Hajj saw in al-'Ayyashi an impediment in his gaining control of Sala, his natural outlet on the ocean. Al-'Ayyashi's persecution of the Andalusians was therefore used as the pretext for fighting him. In 1640 the Dala'iyya army occupied Meknes, which was within al-'Ayyashi's zone of influence. Then after a protracted conflict between al-'Ayyashi's predominantly Arabian army and the Dala'iyya Berbers, the outcome was decided in an engagement on the Sibu river in April 1641. Al-'Ayyashi was killed, and his followers were dispersed...

Al-'Ayyashi's defeat enabled the Dala'iyya to occupy Sala.

...in Sala for ten years after its occupation, the Dala'iyya chief (or sultan as he became called) preserved the Andalusians' autonomy. They knew better how to deal with Europeans, and indirect contacts with the Christians did not unduly compromise the chief's religious standing, while securing the merchandise he needed, especially arms.

In the ten years (1641–51) when the Andalusians controlled Sala under nominal Dala'iyya rule, European agents, sent mostly to deal with questions arising from piracy or connected with commerce, dealt directly with them. From 1643 there was a Dutch consul in

Sala, and in 1648 the French government appointed a substantive consul to reside there, after having been satisfied since 1629 with having a merchant living in Marseilles act as consul while having an agent in Sala. In 1651 Muhammad al-Hajj appointed his son 'Abdulla as governor of Sala. As 'Abdulla also acted as the superintendent of the Dala'iyya state's foreign affairs, his appointment suggests that relations of the Dala'iyya with Europe had become sufficiently important for them to be entrusted to a member of the ruling family. But the Andalusians continued to influence the conduct of foreign relations by acting as interpreters and secretaries, drafting 'Abdulla's letters to foreign rulers and advising him on the treaties he negotiated with some of them.

The most intimate of the Dala'iyya foreign relations was with the Dutch. Lengthy negotiations between 'Abdulla and the Dutch over the provisions of a treaty signed in 1651, and revised in 1655 and 1659, suggest that the Dutch conducted an active trade with Morocco in the 1650's. A recurring problem in these negotiations arose from the dual character of Sala as a centre of trade and a base for piracy. The Dutch were ready to recognize the right of the Sala corsairs to attack the ships of their common Christian enemies, the Spaniards, while obtaining the promise that their own ships would not be molested. At the same time they were opposed to the friendly relations which the Sala pirates and the Dala'iyya chiefs maintained with the rulers of

Algiers. The Algerine pirates were given facilities in Sala, and were allowed to sell their captured goods in it. The attempt by the Dutch to
include in their treaty a provision barring the
Andalusians from cooperating with the
Algerine pirates and trading with Algiers often
led to a deadlock in the negotiations. It is a
revealing indication of the volume of Dutch
trade with Morocco in this period that the
Dutch attitude mellowed whenever the governor of Sala threatened to raise the duties on
exports and imports beyond the customary ten
per cent. [Nasr, pp. 221-2]

The Bou Regreg Republic may have lost some autonomy under the régime of the Dala'iyya, but perhaps gained—
at last—some peace and balance under the nominal *saltanat*
of the Sufi order. In any case, the last two decades of the
Triple Republic were its most golden, at least in terms of
piracy. Freed at last of internecine strife, all three city-states
could turn all their hostility outward—in the corsair holy
war. Moreover, if the corsair republics in their purest form
(1614–1640) were unique as political entities, one can only
use a pleonasm like *"more* unique" to describe the condo-
minium-régime of corsairs and Sufis, which lasted from 1640
to 1660. It boggles the imagination—and indeed it was too
good to last long. The hand of the Dala'iyya and its chief in
Salé—Sidi Abdullah the "prince of Salé"—came to feel heavier and heavier to the Andalusians and pirates. They began
to look for some means to restore their pristine state of total
independence, which by now had come to take on all the
aura of an ancient and revered tradition.

Meanwhile…a disciple of the martyred marabout al-
Ayyashi, an Arab from Larache (and therefore an enemy of
the Dala'iyya Berbers, those "shirtless animals" as one

Islamic historian called them; "beasts unrestrained save by drunkenness or terror," as another put it — with the typical prejudice of urban Arabs), rose up in arms and founded a kingdom of his own in the North. [Coindreau, p. 47; Caillé, p. 222] This man, named Ghailan, looked like a potential savior to the Andalusians of Rabat. They staged an uprising, and beseiged "Prince" Abdullah in the Casbah. The Dala'iyya master M. al-Hajj sent an army to relieve his son, but the army was defeated by Ghailan in June 1660. Abdullah however held on gamely in the Casbah for another year, helped by a shipment of supplies sent by the English governor of Tangiers. At last, in June 1661, he ran out of food and had to surrender the castle.

By this time the Andalusians had come to distrust Ghailan as much as they'd disliked the Dala'iyya — more, in truth. Despite the fact that they'd just run the Dala'iyya out of town, they decided to profess renewed loyalty to the regime in order to stave off Ghailan, lest he prove a worse master. For four years they played hard-to-get, but finally in 1664 capitulated to Ghailan and agreed to pay him the dreaded 10 percent.

Finally, in 1668, the last vestiges of Salé's freedom were wiped out by the rise of the Alawite Dynasty under its Sultan Moulay Raschid, who succeeded in reuniting the whole country for the first time since 1603. The Alawite Sultan had no intention of putting an end to the highly profitable holy war of the Bou Regreg against Europe, and promised the corsairs his protection. Thus, although the Republic had vanished, piracy survived — for a while. Unfortunately the Alawites had huge appetites, and little by little increased the "bite" from 10% to well over half. Eventually the corsairs realized that decent profits were no longer possible. The Moorish pirates stayed on to become captains in the Sultan's "Navy", and perhaps some of the Renegadoes did the same. Others, perhaps, were tempted to move on, to the Carribbean, or to Madagascar, where the pirate scene now began to flourish. The later history of Salé does not concern us, nor the later history of Barbary in general. With the passing of the Republic we lose sight of our Renegadoes—and so, in the next sections, we will return to the heyday (1614–1660) of the Republic, and try to study the Renegadoes themselves, and then the *daily life* of the converts—now that we've looked at their political/military history.

VII

MURAD REIS AND THE
SACK OF BALTIMORE

"We shall have a bon voyago."
—Murad Reis

Much as we might like to meet a whole crew of Sallee
Rovers, people with names, dates, biographies we could
study, "cases" we could analyze in order to better understand
the Renegado character and fate, sadly no such survey will
be possible. If we know little about the converts of Algiers
and Tunis, we know even less about those of Salé. I've won-
dered why this should be so, and can only suggest that Salé
must have been considered (by European travellers and
chroniclers at least) more a backwater than Algiers and
Tunis, perhaps harder to get to, and perhaps even more of a
dangerous hell-hole. Even good Père Dan, who gives us a
brief chapter on Salé, apparently never visited the place but
described it on the basis of hearsay; and the few first-hand
accounts are uninformative. In any case *writers* about Salé—
i.e., literate Europeans—had little curiosity about the
Renegadoes, whom they despised and feared, and represented in the most sensationalistic manner possible. Meanwhile,
those who could tell us something interesting—the converts

themselves—were not *writers*. All categories in which we might discuss the corsairs have been predetermined by outside hostility and propaganda. This is the fate of the revisionist historian attempting to investigate the culture—or the politics of resistance—of a long-vanished non-literate community. Recently, of course, the revisionists themselves have developed (or resurrected) some categories of their own. Marxist or Marxizing historians of "social banditry" and millenialism, like Hobsbawm and Cohn, provide some useful methodology, while writers of a more libertarian-leftist slant (like Hill, Lemisch, Linebaugh, and Rediker) have actually created a whole new historiography of maritime radicalism. But none of them has discussed the Renegadoes. As far as I know, no comparable school of thought has arisen amongst Moroccan or Algerian or Tunisian historians, who *might* have access to untapped documentary resources (assuming such exist); orientalists have ignored the issue, whether out of their own innate cultural conservatism or because no texts can be found; and so the field has been left to us amateur piratologists, *faute de mieux*.

Coindreau (1948: 80–84) has scraped together a brief list of Sallee Rovers from archives and unedited source material in European collections. Thus we have *El Hajj Ali*, probably a Moor, who, on October 14, 1624, off Cape Finistere, captured a Dutch ship under one Captain Euwout Henriexz, during a period when Salé was supposed to be at peace with Holland and therefore ceased to molest its shipping. Hajj Ali demanded that the captain declare himself to be French— and thus a legitimate prize—or else be thrown overboard.

Rais Chafer (Ja'far), an English renegade (mentioned in 1630), *Hassan Ibrahim* (probably native, 1636), and *Maime Rais*, a Dutch renegade (1636). This last, commanding a ship of 200 tons with 13 cannon, captured an English ship and was on his way back to Salé when he himself was taken.

Chaban Rais, Portuguese renegade, in 1646 commanded an Algerian ship, *The Crabbe* (16 cannon and a crew of 175), stopped in Salé to take on stores and arms. At sea for three months, he'd seized nothing better than an English cargo of salt and one fishing boat in the Gulf of Gascony, when (on July 22) he was himself taken by the Dutch pirate Cornelis Verbeck.

Ahmed el-Cortobi, a Spanish renegade (or Morisco?) from Cordoba, was a "fat man." On October 6, 1658, commanding the Saletine ship *The Sun*, he met with a Dutch fleet off Cape Finistere. Again Holland and Salé were supposed to be at peace, and Ahmed Rais decided to pay a friendly visit to the flagship. After returning to his own ship, he watched in horror as one of the Dutch vessels, *The Prophet Daniel* of Lubeck under Captain Pieter Noel, suddenly attacked him. Several corsairs were killed, and the rest—including Ahmed—taken prisoner. The Dutchman then looted *The Sun*, set fire to her, and sank her. This singular event caused a great diplomatic scandal to erupt. Salé demanded recompense, and the Dutch (anxious to preserve the peace) took the affair quite seriously. In January 1659 the Admiralty fined the captain of *The Prophet Daniel* 9,500 florins, and handed over to Salé a vessel equal in tonnage and armament to the sunken *Sun*, while *The Prophet Daniel* itself was awarded to Ahmed el-Cortobi. [Coindreau, 1948: 187]

Ali Campos (Spain), *Case Mareys* (England), and *Courtebey* (the son of Ahmed el-Cortobi, who must have been as "short" as his father was "fat"—unless his name is simply a corruption of Cortobi) are a few more names to add to our list; and *Venetia*, an Italian renegade, famous for his audacity and courage. This fairly exhausts the roster of Renegadoes from the Republican period of Rabat-Salé—with one major exception.

Murad Rais (a.k.a. Morat, John Barber, Captain John,

Caid Morato), the most famous of all Sallee Rovers, was born as Jan Janz in Haarlem, Holland, day and year unknown.

> Jan Jansz began his career, as did most of the Dutch seafaring men who ultimately turned pirates, as a privateer of the States against the Spaniards during the War of Liberation. But this quasi-lawful type of warfare yielded more glory than profit, and Jansz presently trespassed on his commission and found his way to the Barbary coast. There he waged war on the ships of all Christian nations alike, those of Holland not excepted, save that when he attacked a Spaniard he flew the standard of the Prince of Orange as a tribute of sentiment to his origin. When occupied against any other nation's shipping he flew the red half-moon of the Turks. (Gosse, 54-5)[28]

Captured at Lanzarote in 1618 by Barbary Corsairs, Janz apostasized at Algiers—and although the conversion may have been forced, it seems to have taken root, for Murad never begged a pardon or gave the least sign of wishing to return to Christendom. He took up his trade under the leadership of the great Algerian corsair Sulayman Rais (who may also have been Dutch) who died however next year in 1619. Murad provides us with a perfect example of the links between Algiers and Salé, since he now began to move back and forth between them like a man with dual citizenship.

---

28. Coindreau identifies this flag as the 3 gold crescent moons on a red ground often flown by Ottoman privateers and corsairs, but it might also refer to the flag of Salé, showing a gold Man in the Moon on a red ground.

Gosse has this to say about Murad:

> At first he sailed as mate to a famous corsair called Suleiman Reis, of Algiers, but after his chief's death in 1619 settled at Sallee. The port ("its name stunk in all Christendom") was extremely well situated for the new form of piracy, being on the coast of the Atlantic, only fifty miles from Gibraltar, where the corsairs could lie in ambush for everything that passed through the Straits and dash out quickly to meet the East India and Guinea traders. The Sallee fleet was not large, about eighteen all told, and the individual vessels were small, since a bar in the harbour prevented ships of deep draught entering unless they were first unloaded.
>
> The port was nominally subject to the Emperor of Morocco, but shortly after Jansz's arrival the Sallentines declared themselves independent and established what was in effect a pirate republic, governed by fourteen of themselves, with a president who was also the Admiral. The Dutchman was the first to be elected, and to show his adopted countrymen how thoroughly he had become one of themselves he married a Moorish woman, though he had left a wife and family at Haarlem. [Gosse, p. 55]

Other sources say that Murad was appointed Governor of Salé by the Moroccan Sultan Moulay Zaydan in 1624, but this misunderstanding probably arises from the fact that the Sultan, wishing to preserve at least the outward show of sovereignty, merely approved the *fait accompli* of Murad's election. We can assume that Murad was a man of charisma and genuine talent as a leader, and that he had the quality prized by pirates above all others — *luck*. We can assume that he was an enthusiast for the corsair republic, and perhaps its chief ideologue as well as its first elected Admiral. We might even go so far as to assume that a person of such obvious intelligence and courage may have attained a certain degree of political consciousness and revolutionary fervor.

Business prospered under Jansz's efficient administration and he was soon compelled to find an assistant, a post for which he selected a fellow countryman, Mathys van Bostel Oosterlinck. The Vice-Admiral celebrated his appointment by following his superior's example, turning Mohammedan and marrying a Spanish girl of fourteen, although he had a wife and small daughter in Amsterdam.

Jansz, what with prizes taken at sea and his perquisites as Admiral, which included all dues for anchorage, pilotage and other harbor revenues, as well as brokerage on stolen goods, soon became an enormously rich man. Nevertheless he occasionally found the routine of business irksome, the pirate in him asserted itself and he went off on a cruise. During one of these, in November 1622, when he was trying his luck in the English Channel, he ran out of provisions and was forced to put in at the port of Veere in Holland to replenish his stock. It seemed a risky undertaking, but the Admiral of Sallee was a subject of the Emperor of Morocco, who had lately made a treaty with the States of Holland; hence Jan could legally claim the privileges of the port, though the welcome he received was a cold one.

The first visitor to come on board was the Dutch Mrs. Jansz, accompanied by all the little Janszes. "His wife and all his children," a contemporary writer records, "came on board to bid him leave the ship; the parents of the crew did the same but they could not succeed in bringing them to do this as they (the Dutch renegade crew) were too much bitten of the Spaniards and too much hankering after booty." Not only did his crew remain, but it was swelled by recruits, despite a stern order by the magistrates that no one was to take service on the vessel. But times were hard in Holland as a result of nearly half a century of war with Spain; the youth of Veere were more tempted by the opportunity of collecting an easy livelihood while getting in a blow at their old enemy than afraid of magisterial displeasure. Jan left Veere with a great many more hands on board than when he entered it.

A few years later, in mid-winter, Jansz called at Holland again, this time having barely escaped disaster. Off the coast he had met a big ship flying Dutch colors. Jan, momentarily forgetful of treaties, was "at once enamoured of the fine ship and tried to take her"—it was quite probable that after he had succeeded, the lawyers would again enable him to claim the advantage of the treaty. But the affair turned out quite differently: as he came alongside the vessel the Dutch flag was hauled down, the standard of Spain run up in its place and in a moment Spanish troops were swarming on to his deck. The pirates, outclassed, just managed to escape after a bitter fight, many of the crew being killed and wounded. They were glad to get safe into the harbour of Amsterdam.

Jan applied to the authorities for assistance for his sick and wounded but was flatly refused. The unfortunate corsair had meant to violate the treaty, had failed and been punished, and was now receiving further punishment by having its benefits denied him just as if he had succeeded. He was not even granted permission to bury his dead, so the corpses had to be pushed beneath the ice as the only means of disposing of them.

After several comparatively bad years in the Straits of Gibraltar, Jan decided to try his luck where no pirate, Barbary or other, had ever before ventured. In 1627 he engaged as pilot a Danish slave who claimed to have been to Iceland, and instructed him to lead the way to that remote island. Jansz's three ships contained, besides Moors, three English renegades.

The voyage was a daring feat of navigation for the time but the results were not commensurate with the risk. They plundered Reykjavik, the capital, but only obtained some salted fish and a few hides. To make up for their disappointment they caught and brought back four hundred—some say eight—Icelanders: men, women and children.

[Gosse, pp. 55-7]

By 1627 the political situation in Salé had grown a bit warm. The Hornacheros declared their own Republic in the Casbah that year, and al-Ayyashi was actively establishing himself in Old Salé. Murad's Admiralship, which had kept him from sea, may have ended awkwardly; in any case, after his return from Iceland he moved with his Moorish family back to Algiers, and at once resumed the active Corsair life. In 1631 he organized another great adventure, his sacking of the town of Baltimore, County Cork, Ireland.

The real and still unanswered question about the sack of Baltimore is not "how?" Although Murad's seamanship was obviously superb, he was by no means a pioneer in this case, as with Iceland. "Little John" Ward had visited Ireland several times and we can be sure he wasn't the only corsair to follow that route.[29]

The real question about the sack of Baltimore is *"why?"* And for once in our studies, the mists of lost history seem to clear—just a bit—offering us some glimpses of possible motives.

In the first place, Southern and Western Ireland was at this time nearly as infested with pirates as the Barbary Coast. The famous woman pirate Grace O'Malley ruled her own little kingdom in Mayo during the time of Elizabeth, and in fact

29. In fact, as B. Quinn points out in his wonderful book *Atlantean: Ireland's North African and Maritime Heritage*, the raid on Baltimore may be viewed as the last episode of a history stretching back into Neolithic and even Megalithic times. It's interesting to note that the pre-Celtic tribes of Munster were called the Hibernii, assumed to be a branch of the Iberii from Spain; the syllable BER is only one reason (Quinn offers many more) to believe that both peoples were related to the Berbers of North Africa. This opens up a vast and unplowed field for research and speculation on Irish-Moroccan connections, which Quinn has only begun to cultivate. See also Ali and Ali (no date) for an "Afrocentric" treatment of the same theme.

had paid that ruler a kind of state visit, queen-to-queen, in 1593. [Chambers, 1979. Elizabeth and Grace got on very well—kindred spirits, no doubt.] As for County Cork, we learn (from a rather rare book, *Pirate Harbours and Their Secrets*, by B. Fuller and R. Leslie-Melville):

> Sir William Herbert, the Vice-President of Munster, summed up the state of the province in 1589 in these words: "If piracies be there maintained, and every port and haven in those parts be made acceptable for them, we must give over our inhabitation there, since we shall pass neither our commodities or ourselves over the seas, but at their mercy. The province generally is made a receptacle of pirates. They are too much favoured in Kerry. Sir Edward Denny has received Gascon wine which was robbed from Frenchmen, and Lany Denny has received goods which were taken from 'Brittaines.' One Captain Maris, of Youghal, a known negotiator in these kinds of affairs, is shortly to remove to Tawlaght, a castle of Sir Edward Denny's, near Tralee, there to exercise that trade." Denny, later created Earl of Norwich, also had seats in Cornwall, and was therefore a neighbour to the Killigrews. He, in fact, did for the pirates in Ireland what the Killigrews and Sir John Perrot did for them in Cornwall and South Wales. When influential noblemen acted as "fences" piracy was certainly a paying game... As the Royal Navy was practically non-existent until the latter half of the century, when James II placed it on a sound basis, it was virtually impossible "to eye and awe the inhabitants from traffic with these

caterpillars," to use the picturesque words of Lord Danvers.

The extent to which the pirates held the upper hand may be judged from the fact that early in 1609 Danvers himself was blockaded in Cork by four sail of pirates carrying some three hundred men. The Lord-President could not raise even one ship strong enough to defy the marauders, and so in Cork he had to stay, while the unwelcome visitors sailed up and down the coast seeking sustenance. So as to prevent them re-victualling in Co. Kerry, the supplies of corn which were usually exported from Co. Cork were held up, but this seems to have annoyed the inhabitants far more than the pirates.

Later in the year an even greater force of pirates, numbering eleven ships and 1,000 men, assembled off the coast. [This was Captain Ward and his fleet from Tunis.] Sir Richard Moryson, then the Vice-President of Munster, was powerless to take action against them, and had to fall back on the old and obviously unsatisfactory method of pardoning them. "The continual repair of the pirates to the western coast of the province," he told Lord Salisbury, "in consequence of the remoteness of the place, the wildness of the people, and their own strength and wealth, both to command and entice relief, is very difficult for us to prevent or remedy."

Such was the position of affairs when Berehaven first attracted the angry attention of the English Government. This was in the days of Donnell O'Sullivan Beare. As a haven the spot was and still is ideal. In proof of this it is necessary to say no more than that it is one of the naval bases retained by Great Britain under the Treaty of 1921. It is really a haven within a haven, for it lies far into Bantry Bay, which itself is famous as one of the world's finest natural harbours as well as a very beautiful one.

Even in the middle of the eighteenth century it could be said that Bantry Bay was large enough to hold all the shipping in Europe, and the statement was by no means absurd, for the Bay is about twenty-one miles long and averages three miles in width. Moreover, it is deep. Berehaven is formed by Bere Island, a humpbacked strip of land about seven miles long and one-and-a-half wide, which lies off the northern shore of Bantry Bay. Seen from the head of the Bay, that is to say from its eastern end, the island bears a striking resemblance to a basking crocodile. Lying as it does roughly parallel to the mainland, and almost joining it at its seaward end, the island affords shipping a perfect haven of refuge when Bantry Bay itself is lashed into fury.

Donnell O'Sullivan's chief stronghold was Dunboy Castle, on the mainland and commanding the narrow seaward entrance to the haven. He was a wild sea-rover, bold in the knowledge of the strength of his lair and in the backing of the powerful O'Sullivan clan to which the district belonged. Even to-day at least seventy-five percent of the inhabitants of Castletown Bere, the remote little town on the mainland opposite the island, are O'Sullivans. Here came pirates great and small, and a merry trade they ran, for Berehaven had a rival for their favours, the neighbouring harbour of Baltimore known also by the picturesque name of Dunashad, or the Fort of the Jewels. Dunashad Haven is a sheltered bay "where infinate number of ships may ride, having small tides, deep water, and a good place to careen ships," to quote Sir Thomas Stafford.

The haven is formed by Sherkin Island, which acts as a natural breakwater. Further out to sea is Clear Island, the nearest land to the Fasnet Rock Lighthouse, whose powerful beam has cheered many a transatlantic traveller. This well-sheltered lair and the surrounding district, then the largest barony in Ireland, was run by the O'Driscolls who, perhaps, deserve to be remembered as the most notable clan of Irish sea-rovers. Rich pickings were to be had from the pirates who came running before favourable winds with prizes snatched from the hands of the hated English. And so it is to be supposed that little affection existed between the O'Sullivans and the O'Driscolls. It cannot be doubted that the pirates were well aware of this fact and made excellent capital from their knowledge.

Thus Berehaven and Baltimore were not pirate lairs in the sense that they were owned by self-confessed sea-robbers who used them as an essential base for their operations. They were useful stations into which any pirate could sail to secure a long price for his cargoes or retreat for protection if hard pressed. At the same time, there is no doubt that the owners of both harbours did a certain amount of pirating on their own accounts and that they were not foolishly particular in the matter of infringing each other's interests, or the interests of any other Irishmen. There was, for instance, the occasion when Sir Fineen O'Driscoll — Sir Fineen of the Ships, as he was known — burnt his fingers badly over a cargo of rich wine.

One stormy February day this worthy, in company with his bastard son, Gilly Duff, nicknamed the Black Boy, saw a ship beating about helplessly at the entrance to Baltimore Bay. Jumping into a boat the thoughtful pair offered to pilot the stranger, much to the relief of the harassed sailors. She was a Portuguese vessel laden with one hundred tuns of wine consigned to certain merchants in Waterford. All this the O'Driscolls very soon found out, and they determined to make the valuable cargo their own. The Portuguese captain was delighted when the charming strangers asked him and his officers to dine with them in their haven. Apparently he suspected nothing when the crew were included in the invitation. It was a case of the spider and the fly. No sooner were the sailors inside the castle than they were seized and clapped into irons, and the work of transferring the wine began. But the Waterford merchants were not the men to have their pride (and their pockets) hurt in this way, and they speedily fitted out an armed vessel to avenge their loss.

The O'Driscolls, still dismantling the wine-ship, were surprised, and barely escaped with their lives. Flushed with the victory, the Mayor of Waterford sent another expedition some days later, and they laid Baltimore Castle in ruins besides burning all O'Driscoll's ships, about fifty in number. His own galley of thirty oars they towed back to Waterford as evidence of their prowess. Baltimore Haven did not take long to recover from this reverse. Fresh wealth flowed in readily enough from trade with the pirates.

The people of Berehaven were not behindhand in turning their attention to any scheme that would make them money. Their pride, if not their self-interest, would not allow them to play second fiddle to Baltimore. So Donnell O'Sullivan added to his activities as "fence" on a grand scale by leasing fishing rights to foreigners. And, strangely enough, the rights he hired out were for the most part his own to sell. "The coast yields such abundance of sea fish as few places in Christendom do the like," wrote Sir Thomas Stafford, "and at the fishing time there was such a resort of fishermen of all nations, although the duties which they paid unto O'Sullivan was very little yet at the least it was worth unto him £1500 yearly." Today the equivalent sum would be at least £15,000.

So continued the rivalry between the two pirate lairs for many years. But Berehaven was the first to fall. On September 16th, 1602, Sir George Carew opened a fierce attack upon the castle of Dunboy. The siege formed part of the

General's ruthless suppression of the rebellion of 1600–1603. At the time the haven was garrisoned by one hundred and twenty men only, and Carew's forces numbered at least five thousand, but the gallant defenders held out until the 18th, when the walls were finally breached and the attackers burst in. Even at the very last moment, when the Royalists were inside the castle, the Irish nearly achieved a pyrrhic victory. As the soldiers burst into the magazine they saw Richard MacGeoghegan, the gallant commander of the castle, painfully crawling towards a number of powder barrels with a lighted candle in his hand. They seized him in the nick of time, and although he was mortally wounded, killed him out of hand in a fit of senseless and disgusting brutality.

O'Sullivan himself was fighting elsewhere, and managed to escape to Spain, only to be treacherously stabbed to death by an Anglo-Irishman. As a pirate den, Berehaven may have thoroughly deserved suppression, but Carew did not attack it on this score. He punished the pirates for their alleged disloyalty to the Crown, a matter which was by no means proven. Consequently, the wholesale slaughter which accompanied the capture of Dunboy Castle is a matter which Englishmen prefer to forget. It was unnecesary, unworthy, and unjustified. Only a crumbling fragment now remains of Dunboy Castle, and the point on which it stood is overgrown with trees. Thus fell Berehaven for a time.

[Fuller and Leslie-Melville, 1935: 168–173]

As for Baltimore, we are indebted for its story to an Irish source, "The Sack of Baltimore" by H. Barnby (1969). Sir Fineen O'Driscoll "Of the Ships," who appears as an engaging rogue in *Pirate Harbours*, now takes on a less romantic air. He turns out to be a collaborator with the English; he sided with them in the Desmond Rebellion. He turned several "murderers" (rebels?) over to the authorities, and was so deeply in debt he began to sell leases on parts of his demesne to English colonists. His Irish subjects were left to fend for themselves.

In 1605 an Englishman named Thomas Crooke offered to purchase a lease for twenty-one years of the town of Baltimore and its surrounding ploughlands for £2,000. Sir Fineen O'Driscoll accepted his offer and the lease was drawn up. Surprisingly, there is no record of there having been any complaint from the existing townsfolk. It is possible that by 1605 many Baltimore residents, offended by the presence of English troops in the area, may have moved away to the north or to the comparative sanctuary of one of the larger islands of Roaring Water Bay.

When Thomas Crooke purchased his lease from Sir Fineen O'Driscoll in 1605, the English physical presence in West Cork was very small and his scheme to plant several hundred English settlers in the Baltimore area must have been highly acceptable to the authorities in Cork, Dublin and Westminster. If however these same authorities had stopped to ask themselves how such a considerable party of settlers were to maintain themselves in this area, they might have come to some slightly disturbing conclusions. In the words of the old saying, "the law ends at Leap." In the Calendar of State Papers, Ireland, 1606–1608, there are twenty-one references to Baltimore and most of these refer to piracy.

However, the formal establishment of the English plantation at Baltimore went steadily ahead. On 3 July 1607 Baltimore was authorised by "His Majesties High Court of Chancery…to hold…a Friday Market, and two Fairs on 24 June and 28 October and two days after each…" On 26 September 1612 the borough received its official charter. This appointed "…Thomas Crooke, Esq., to be the first Soveraigne, and James Salmon, Daniel Leach, Joseph Carter, William Hudson, Joseph Hoskins, Stephen Hunt, Thomas Bennett, the elder, Thomas Bennett, the younger, Roger Bennett, William Howling, Thomas Germon, and Richard Commy to be the first twelve burgesses…." The sovereign was to hold court for minor offences and civil actions every Friday, while he and his council were empowered to establish byelaws. They were also invested with the duty of electing two discreet men to attend the parliament that James I was planning to summon at Dublin in the near future. Thomas Crooke had been appointed the first sovereign, but for the future, the burgesses were to meet once a year for the especial purpose of electing one of their own number to hold this office.

Those Irish who remained to mingle with

the new planters appear to have been quite prepared to put up with any sort of change. However not many elected to remain and a Spaniard who came into Baltimore harbour on a ship in 1608 was told that there were now very few Irish there.

Thomas Crooke's achievement was remarkable. He had, in the words of the Lord Bishop of Cork, "...at his own charges...gathered out of England a whole town of English people, larger and more civilly and religiously ordered than any town in this province that began so lately...."

The reliable Anglican theology of the new West Cork planters enabled the representatives of King James to overlook less attractive features about Thomas Crooke's new plantation. It seems more than possible that Thomas Crooke established his plantation at Baltimore with the intention of trading with pirates. This does not imply that the planters there were to occupy themselves with no other activities, but they were a sea-harbour settlement and relied on visiting ships to purchase their produce and skills in return for money or trade goods. The way in which their customers had acquired money and trade goods was no concern of theirs. The new planters at Baltimore were behaving in exactly the same manner as many harbours in southwest England had behaved for decades, but England under a legalistically-minded king was becoming unsafe for pirates. Thomas Crooke had foreseen this situation developing and had taken steps to profit by it.

The official trade carried through Baltimore was ludicrously small. According to one source, only three ship loads of wine entered the harbour during 1614 and 1615. The unofficial trade must have been considerable. Certainly pirates' goods brought into Ireland through Baltimore were supplied throughout the province and the president of Munster himself and many other leading citizens of Cork are known to have bought from that source. By 1608, no more than two years after the establishment of the English at Baltimore, Thomas Crooke was called before the Privy Council in London to answer charges of having had dealings with pirates. It was this charge that prompted the bishop of Cork's letter of recommendation. The Privy Council acquitted him with all honour; how could they do otherwise? There had been revolts before in Munster, in which English planters had had their throats cut. If ambitious, energetic men such as Richard Boyle and Thomas Crooke were able to persuade large parties of Protestant English to go and colonise this uncertain area, how could the English authorities jeopardize their enterprise by being too nice about their trading methods?

The Privy Council may have acquitted Thomas Crooke and his fellow planters but others were less complaisant. By 1608 the Venetians were writing that there were two chief nests of English pirates, and one of these was on the Irish coast at Baltimore. An English source stated during 1608 that all the harbours of Munster were safe for pirates but that Baltimore was most frequented by them. Also during 1608 the president of Munster wrote that Robinson, a pirate, arrived at Baltimore in a ship of one hundred and twenty tons and twenty cannon. "...At first his strict directions being observed by those that inhabit about Baltimore...although they could not be denied ordinary relief by the weak inhabitants, yet they were hindered for a while from the commodities that might repair their defects; until, daily re-inforcing themselves with fresh men, they grew so fearful to the fishermen and all the country, that having neither means to defend their own nor to offend them he was forced to confirm a treaty...with them...." Since the king's chief officer in the province of Munster confirms having dealings with a pirate at Baltimore, it is reasonable to assume that the inhabitants of that place, surrounded by a still largely Gaelic hinterland and with the nearest officer of the Crown many miles away, would have been ready and willing to trade.

They had ways also of covering their actions with a semblance of legality. One of the most successful pirates of this time was a man named Henry Mainwaring. He had accepted a pardon from the King and wrote a most comprehensive work on the methods employed by pirates on the coast of Ireland. He states that when pirates needed supplies of meat they would send a discreet man on shore to seek out a farmer with cattle for sale. The farmer would say where he would put the cattle and the pirates would send a party of men ashore to fetch them after dark. These would fire off a musket or two as though they were making a land raid. The local people, amply forwarned, would keep well out of the way. The business was very welcome, said Mainwaring, because cattle sold by this means usually fetched double their market value.

The new English plantation at Baltimore seems to have flourished. King James, embarrassed by the complaints of foreign merchants, insisted on steps being taken to suppress the pirates of south-west Ireland. Once in a while a royal man-o-war sailed along the coast. But the royal ships were ususally old and badly maintained. The pirates, whose necks depended on their agility, used small Dutch-built warships which, when regularly defouled, were the swiftest sailors afloat. They seldom allowed themselves to be caught by the royal ships, and if caught, they often seem to have managed to come to an understanding with their captors. Many pirates were operating but very few were hanged. The Dutch obtained King James's permission to search the creeks and harbours of south-west Ireland for pirates, but when they appeared off Baltimore and asked for a pilot to bring them into the harbour, Thomas Crooke told them to be off. This would seem to be a very high line to take with the commander of a Dutch squadron operating with royal permission; but Thomas Crooke must have known what he was doing because he continued to prosper. It is only possible to guess the extent of his financial prosperity, but we know that he became a baronet in 1624 shortly before he died.

The new English community at Baltimore was almost entirely the product of the enterprise, energy and lack of scruple of Sir Thomas Crooke, Bart. It is therefore strangely appropriate that things should have started to go wrong almost from the time of his death.

It seems possible, and in fact is assumed by some writers (e.g. *Pirate Harbours*), that after Crooke's death the people of Baltimore decided to go straight. Their pilchard fisheries were proving remarkably profitable, and the authorities were slowly increasing their control over the "lawless" regions. We may hypothesize that in 1624 the leaders of Baltimore made it known on the pirate grapevine that the days of hospitality were over, and the port closed to all illegality save a bit of harmless smuggling.

Meanwhile the feckless Sir Fineen had sunk himself even deeper in the mire of debt. A creditor appeared on the scene.

Sir Walter Coppinger, Bart., was a magistrate at Cork City whose acquisitiveness bore a marked resemblance to the swashbuckling behaviour of his Viking forefathers. He recognised just as clearly as Richard Boyle or Thomas Crooke that West Cork was underpopulated and ripe for development. He was, however, a staunch Roman Catholic and no lover of the new English Protestants that were beginning to settle the land. He had no wish to plant Englishmen in West Cork. His interest was in building up his personal estate in this area. His original acquisitions were mainly from the old Irish proprietors; sometimes their title was confused and Sir Walter found himself in dispute with other occupants. On these occasions his manners could be rough. The London East India Company purchased woods high up the tidal estuary of the Bandon river in 1612. Here they began to build ships. Sir Walter chose to believe the land belonged to him. He did not care to see Englishmen cutting down his trees so he set armed men to harry them. These hired muscle-men terrified the shipyard workmen and broke down the dams that had been built to operate the hammer mills. The dispute over Dun Daniel woods subsided into oblivion, but Sir Walter was soon appearing in the records again. He next made an attempt to take over Baltimore. His claim was not a frivolous one.

In 1573 Fineen O'Driscoll had surrendered his lands to the English Crown along with other tribal lords of Munster. This was part of a complicated land title reform the net result of which was that Sir Fineen now held title to his lands in person and not, as previously, merely in his condition as elected leader of the Sept. Fineen had been a young man when he took this step; for many years the change had no practical effect and his life in West Cork continued in its normal pattern. In 1583 he visited London and received his knighthood. As Sir Fineen O'Driscoll his standard of living may well have proved more expensive. In 1602, his prestige suffered a serious blow when he was obliged to hand over three of his castles to the English, but his writ still ran in West Cork and in the same year he detained and handed over to the English authorities wanted murderers who had sought refuge in his territories. However, his financial position seems to have deteriorated sharply about then and one of the immediate results of this was his sale of a twenty–one–year lease of Baltimore to Thomas Crooke in 1605.

About 1616 it seems likely that Sir Walter Coppinger lent Sir Fineen O'Driscoll a sum of money on security of his lands occupied by the plantation at Baltimore. Sir Thomas Crooke had purchased the lease of Baltimore only for twenty-one years. The purchase had been made in 1605, which meant that in 1626 the lease either had to be renegotiated or the use of the property returned to Sir Fineen, his heirs or assignees. If Sir Fineen did not repay the loan, Sir Walter Coppinger automatically became his assignee and the absolute owner of Baltimore on expiry of the lease. In the meantime he demonstrated the firmness of his intentions by harrying the English planters in every way that he was able. At first [Sir Walter] used force but the planters seem to have soon organised themselves adequately for their own defence; accordingly, he altered his tactics and began to institute civil and criminal actions against individual planters in rapid succession. As a magistrate of long standing in Cork city, Sir Walter must have made a disturbing opponent.

Sir Thomas Crooke died in 1624 and the Baltimore plantation lost its main guide and sponsor. In 1626 the lease held from Sir Fineen came to its end and the land and buildings occupied by the English at Baltimore would fall into the hands of that inveterate opponent of the new English, Sir Walter Coppinger. The planters applied to the House of Lords for relief. This was a shrewd move, for the English authorities were obviously going to be most reluctant to see a Protestant English plantation, so strategically placed in the remote south western parts of Ireland, fall into the hands of a Roman Catholic gentleman of doubtful loyalty. Negotiations were set in hand. It is not known what form these took but there were certain results. On 14 April 1629 a deed of defeasance was signed by Sir Fineen and Sir Walter. The result of this was that the English planters remained in undisturbed possession of their leasehold property at Baltimore, although Sir Walter got possession of the fort of Dún na Séad. [Barnby, 1969]

So—to sum up—in 1629 the creditor Sir Walter Coppinger was bilked of possession of Baltimore. Sir Walter hated the English, and had used violence against them several times. He hated the people of Baltimore because they had successfully resisted his advances, and because they were Imperialist Protestants. Sir Walter had two very good motives—in his own mind at least—for doing an injury to that little colony—patriotism and profit. Two years later, a great injury did in fact befall Baltimore. *Cui bono?*, as the lawyers say.

In late April or early May 1631, Morat Rais sailed from Algiers with two well-armed ships probably of Dutch construction. They are reported to have taken "...9 Portingales, 3 Pallicians (?), 17 Frenchmen..." and to have sunk two French ships after thoroughly looting them, before reaching British waters. Then, on 17 June an English ship of about 60 tons was seized half way between Lands End and the coast of Ireland. The name of the master of this ship was Edward ffawlett and he had with him a crew of nine men. Morat treated this ship exactly as he had dealt with the French coasters. This seems, at first glance, to have been a gross waste of valuable hulls. North African corsairs, however, were men with a keen sense of values and they would certainly have had good reason for so disposing of hardly acquired assets. The three small vessels may all have been old and in a state of bad repair, or else too slow to keep up with the swift sailing Dutch ships. Also, they were probably considered too weak to stand much chance of reaching Algiers unescorted. A prize crew of renegade seamen and Turkish soldiers attempting to sail back to Algiers in ships this size stood a strong chance of being picked up near the Straits of Gibraltar by some Catholic warship and of ending their days chained to a galley oar.

Morat's two ships continued northwesterly towards the Irish coast. He and probably some of his crew still had bitter memories of being badly mauled by a Spanish warship off the Dutch coast. The English Channel and North Sea certainly teemed with valuable merchant ships but it also teemed with warships — Charles I was interested in the royal navy and was building it up once again.

The two Algerian warships made landfall off the Old Head of Kinsale on the morning of 19 June and it was here they scooped up two fishing boats working out of Dungarvan harbour. These boats were too small even for Morat and his crew to have any interest in plundering and they took them purely for the sake of the information they could yield.

The captain of one of these boats was a Roman Catholic named Hackett. From now on, keep an eye on this man. Everything he does looks suspicious.

Morat's ships would have been like hundreds of other vessels busy about the coastal waters of northern Europe. So there was nothing to alarm the two fishing boats from Dungarvan. By the time Hackett and his men became apprehensive, it would have been too late to escape. The red felt caps and embroidered red waistcoats of the Janissaries would have soon told them who their captors were. They were ordered up into Morat's ship, while their own fishing boat under a prize crew rowed in pursuit of the other mackerel fishermen.

The Algerians' voyage had lasted for perhaps two months and all the booty they had to show for their trouble was a few mackerel, a quantity of indifferent ship's stores and forty captive seamen. This was small loot when it had to be divided between two hundred and eighty hungry men; particularly so when half had to go to the owners of the man-o-war and a further twenty to twenty-five percent to the militia and customs officers of Algiers.

There would probably have been renegades or even Christian slaves among Morat's crew who would have known Kinsale. These men may well have urged their captain to sail into Kinsale harbour on the chance of finding a rich ship or two lying at anchor. But when Morat ordered John Hackett to pilot them in to the landlocked anchorage, the Dungarvan man told them that Kinsale would be too hot for them. As an alternative he suggested attacking Baltimore. One wonders why.

Dungarvan lay to the east of Kinsale. It may therefore have seemed a good idea to Hackett to persuade the Algerians to move westerly. Baltimore was the first harbour of any size west of Kinsale. It also had a reputation as a place of refuge for English pirates and it might have seemed only just to Hackett to encourage dog to eat dog. But probably the major reason why John Hackett suggested Baltimore was that it was a comparatively new English Protestant plantation.

It strikes me—and this is only a hypothesis—that

Hackett might have had a "deeper" reason for his odd behavior. All that we know about him derives from his own testimony at his trial, when presumably he was trying to justify his actions with some cover story. What if the "scooping up" of Hackett's vessel off Kinsale was not an accident but a *rendezvous*? What if Hackett, a Catholic, were an agent of the Catholic Sir Walter Coppinger? What if Coppinger had been in touch with corsair representatives—easy enough in County Cork, it would seem—and had suggested a raid on Baltimore? Perhaps he painted it as a richer prize than it proved in fact, or perhaps he sweetened the suggestion with an offer of payment—he could afford it. And maybe on June 19 Hackett deliberately put his boat in the way of "capture", so he could act as pilot and guide to the corsairs. (We know the corsairs *always* sought out such experts, like the Moriscos who acted as spies in Spain, or the Danish slave who guided Murad to Iceland.) A lot of pure conjecture, of course. But…keep an eye on Hackett.

> The two Algerian ships headed westerly. The first place at which they were recorded as being noticed from the shore was at Castlehaven, five miles east of Baltimore. They were seen here to sail past the entrance to the anchorage at sunset, but their appearance caused no alarm.
>
> Darkness was just falling when the two ships dropped anchors off the entrance to Baltimore harbour. Their exact position was reported as one musket shot to the south-east of this entrance.
>
> It was ten o'clock on a Sunday evening and most people were already at home, if not actually in bed. The two Algerian ships, swinging to

the movement of the tide at their anchor cables, were as unseen and unsuspected as if they had still been secured to the Mole at Algiers.

Morat made his decision without delay. He took one of the ship's rowing boats and led a reconnaissance into the harbour. For guide, he took Captain ffawlett, master of the English ship he had seized near Lands End. This proves that the English captain must have visited Baltimore before, probably with cargoes of contraband wine from Spain or south-west France. With strips of sacking tied round the boat's oars to deaden the sound of rowing the reconnaissance party moved quietly along the broken shore line of the harbour, while Captain ffawlett pointed out the lie of the land and the main parts of the township. Morat soon made up his mind. "We shall have a bon voyago," he announced to his waiting crew when he returned to his ship and he immediately outlined his plan of action.

A landing like this from the sea by the Algerians was always the same. It depended on causing panic, and panic comes more easily in the chill hours before dawn. At two a.m., the large landing party clambered down from the two ships and crowded into the rowing boats and the two fishing boats that they had towed from Kinsale. The Janissaries carried muskets and scimitars, the rest had armed themselves with long knives and carried iron crow bars and tar-soaked strips of canvas wrapped round long sticks ready for lighting. John Hackett accompanied the landing party, a point which must have told heavily against him at his subsequent trial. A man could possibly be forced to point out the lie of the land from a rowing boat by having a knife held against his ribs. But for so recent a captive to accompany a landing party with its distinct possibilities of escape strongly implies some special understanding with his captors. The boats followed one after the other between the points of Sherkin Island and the mainland. They gave a wide berth to the rock on the east side of the harbour entrance which showed its presence by a slight surge and break in the ground swell. The dark file moved Northwards to Coney Island, skirted along the small cliffs, then swung round into the sheltered semi-circle that is the Cove. The boats picked their way between the anchored fishing craft and ran up on to the mud and gravel beach. The invaders lit their firebrands and then with a concerted shout they leapt from their boats and ran up the beach.

Today there are only a few houses at the Cove, but the stone foundations of many more can still be seen in the fields overlooking the water. In 1631, most would have been thatched with straw and built of wood and plaster, or of rubble packed between wood and plaster shuttering. These houses were probably extremely damp, but in June their roof timbers, at least, would have been dry enough to burn. Suddenly there was noise, light, and confusion erupting in the peace of a summer night. But there was little killing. Dead bodies have no value, and the Corsairs seldom forgot their commercial interests.

Speed was all-important. The night was dark for the invaders too. They could only guess at what was lying just outside the circle of light thrown by their burning brands. They knew that it was unlikely that there were many armed men within close quarters, but they could not be sure. They had no wish to delay any longer than was quite necessary. It is not known whether the tide was rising or falling at the time, but Morat Rais was seaman enough to have made sure that competent men had been left with his boats to keep them in readiness. The captives were driven down to the shore and herded into the Algerians' boats....

Morat Rais decided that the main part of the village was worth an attack. There was an element of risk involved, he knew, and he made his plans with this in mind. Accompanied by the curious John Hackett, who was putting the rope more securely round his neck with every step, he led a party of men towards the fort and jetty. Halfway along this narrow track the hillside slopes steeply in above it. Here he left sixty of his musketeers in position dominating the track and foreshore. He then continued to the main village accompanied by men equipped for the assault.

The attack on the first houses proceeded smoothly; the firebrands set the roofs alight, the crowbars tore open the wooden doors. The official account claimed that the Algerians broke open forty houses in the main part of

Baltimore, looted thirty-seven and took ten captives. Obviously the element of surprise had been lost. There must have been many more than ten people among thirty-seven houses; the others must have had ample warning to escape. The hillside slopes gently upwards from the empty fort. Here, where there were more homesteads, one of the planters, William Harris, was taking defensive measures. Already he had fired a number of random shots from his musket, while one of his neighbors had started to beat a drum.

Morat Rais would have noted all these signs. He probably found the beating of the drum the most disturbing. Drums make martial music and are usually carried by soldiers. He ordered his men to withdraw to the boats. They obeyed promptly, went quickly back along the track, collected their musketeers waiting in ambush, and continued down to the Cove. They boarded the waiting boats and pulled away from shore. The next terra firma they would touch would be the dry soil of Africa.

The list contained in the official records is not exactly clear. It gives both names and numbers in some detail but its wording is slightly ambiguous. Yet James Frizell, reporting on the arrival of the Baltimore captives at Algiers on 10 August gives the figure as eighty-nine women and children and twenty men, two more than listed as officially having been taken from Baltimore. The official list names two men killed in the raid, and two elderly captives sent ashore when Hackett and one of his fellow Dungarvan fishermen were released together with ffawlett the Cornish sea captain.

So it seems only the *Celts* were set free! Irish and Cornish "prisoners" released, and *English captives* taken back to Algiers! And above all, the ubiquitous Hackett, so informative, so...*enthusiastic* about this chance to cooperate with Moorish corsairs! He would have done better to stick with Murad and flee to Algiers. But presumably he had reasons to remain in Ireland—perhaps to report to Sir Walter? To be paid off?

An amusing account survives in English official archives, describing the futile attempt to pursue Morat Rais:

> On the day aforesaid before yt was light news came to one Thomas Bennett by some that escaped of the first surprisal who presently poasted a letter to Mr. James Salmon of Castlehavn praying him to use his best endeavours to persuade Mr. Pawlett who then lay in the harbour with his shipp, to hast to the rescue of the foresaid captives, who yt seems could not prevail; Then Mr. Salmon presently with all speed sent to Captaine Hooke, Captn of the king's shipp, then ryding in the harbour of Kinsale, informing of the proceedings and Sir Samuell Crooke likewise sent a letter to the Soveraigne of Kinsale, manifesting the calamityes aforesaid, and praying him to hasten the Captain of the king's shipp to their rescue; Mr. Salmon's man by his direction, went also from Kinsale to Mallow, to informe the Lord President of the proceedings who presently sent his comand to the Soveraigne of Kinsale;

and Captaine Hooke to set forth with the king's shipp, and to hasten her to the service, who came accordingly within four days. But the Turks having not continued in the harbor longer than they could bring in their anchors, and hoyst sayle, were gotten out of view, and the king's shipp followed after them, but could never get sight of them. [Sir Samuel Crooke must be the heir of the late Sir Thomas Crooke.]

And so, by Hooke or by Crooke, the pirates got clean away. (Hooke's head later rolled, since apparently the buck stopped with him, and he was blamed for the whole debacle, as we shall see.)

Barnby does an excellent job of tracing the fate of the prisoners of Baltimore.

There is no record left of this journey but, by comparing the accounts left by the Icelandic captives with two other contemporary descriptions of voyages in Algerian ships, it is possible to form some idea of the conditions with which the Baltimore people had to contend.

The men were confined in the ship's hold, along with the English and French seamen taken earlier in the voyage and the ten or so Dungarvan fishermen. All were fettered, or else had their legs confined in wooden stocks. According to one Icelandic account the male captives were released from their chains when the ships were well away from land.

The women and children were not fettered or chained. In fact they were free to go anywhere that they wished on the ship, except the quarter deck; to set foot here they had to wait for an invitation. The Icelanders reported that Morat's men made a great fuss of the children while the Turks particularly were often to be seen giving them titbits of food from their own private stores. The Icelandic parson who left the most detailed account of the voyage, described how, when his wife gave birth to a baby during the course of their voyage, two of the renegade seamen each gave her one of their shirts to use as swaddling cloths. This same account says that the ship's officers issued the women with lengths of canvas so that they could erect temporary cabins between decks and thus enjoy some sort of privacy. It is reasonable to assume that the Baltimore women were granted the same consideration.

The Algerian ships had been at sea for many weeks. The Turks of Algiers and their renegade seamen had a fearsome reputation in Christian Europe for savagery and lechery towards women and boys, and they retained this reputation until the last days of their existence in Africa. Yet neither the accounts of the Icelanders nor any other contemporary accounts of similar voyages mention women captives being molested in any way. This could mean, possibly, that molestation was taken for granted and not considered worth mentioning; but the Icelandic parson did write in his account that the Algerian renegades had raped one Icelandic girl while they were ashore on the Vestmanna Islands, and what is worth a mention ashore is surely worth a word afloat. Europeans writing from Algiers were always ready to describe the sufferings of Christian captives in affecting terms, yet the English Consul James Frizell writing from Algiers about the arrival of the Baltimore captives, mentioned no complaint by the women....

The total human booty that Morat Rais had brought back from his voyage was not outstandingly large. Two hundred and eighty men had been away from the city for something like three months and had returned with twenty men and eighty-seven women and children from Baltimore; nine Irish fishermen, nine English sailors from Captain ffawlett's ship, about seventeen French sailors, nine Portuguese and three other sailors. This adds up to one hundred and fifty-four bodies the proceeds from which had to be divided among all members of the crew plus a great many other financially interested people. It was probably already mid-morning by the time this rather pathetic squad was led off the Mole, through the harbour gate and into the city.

The new captives were brought to the Bashaw's palace. Fifteen of Morat Rais's captives belonged to the Bashaw by right. It was doubtless a dramatic and pathetic moment when this fifteen were separated from their fellows. The Algerians were not sentimental about captives. The Bashaw would have chosen those slaves that pleased him most, and if this meant that he was separating one member of a family from another, it would have been a matter of no importance to him. Père Dan the French Redemptionist priest who reached Algiers in 1635 said that it had been a pitiful sight to see the Irish families separated, while the nine year old son of the Icelandic Parson captured in 1627 was sold separately from his parents and sent to Tunis.

The British consul, James Frizell, must certainly have visited the captives from Baltimore shortly after their arrival at Algiers for he wrote during August 1631 to the Secretary of State for Foreign Affairs in London that "107 prisoners had arrived of which 20 were men and the rest women and children...." At least this establishes that they all survived the voyage. They were more fortunate in this respect than the Icelanders had been four years previously, amongst whom there had been four deaths at sea. James Frizell was a sparse letter writer; having stated that the captives from Baltimore were alive, he asked for funds to be sent to enable him to arrange their ransom, and left it at that. He gave no details of their experiences when they reached the city.

We know that the one hundred and seven men, women and children who were surprised from their modest beds between two and four in the morning on the 20 June 1631 had reached Algiers in safety. They were then exposed on the open market before hundreds of alien eyes, and were sold and delivered over to their purchasers. There is no record left of their sale and purchase. No one actually knows the fate of any of the Baltimore captives. However, bearing in mind the recorded experiences of other Algerian captives at about this time, it is possible to speculate with some confidence on their fate.

At Algiers a slave had four potential sources of value; as a labourer, as a companion, as a source of income or as a step towards paradise. The first category included all men of strength, able to haul an oar, to dig a drain, carry a load, work in the fields or labour in the city's stone quarries. Also included in this category were the women captives considered to be fit only for domestic drudgery.

The second category included all those Christian slaves who were purchased to serve as companions to their owners, personable young males to be employed as pages and young women to fill the role of concubines.

The third class comprised all captives of wealth or particular skill. These captives were usually purchased as a speculation, large sums being paid on the expectation that their ransom would in a short time yield an even larger return. Jewish and Italian merchants in Algiers would, on appropriate references, lend captives funds to purchase their own redemptions, the debt to be repaid in due course in their country of origin. This was a much sought after trade as it meant good profits and a rapid turn-over for everyone. A skilled captive was a long-term investment. Generally his purchaser would advance him sufficient funds to purchase the tools of his trade and to set up a workshop.

This sum would then be added to a redemption price and the captive would be free to follow his trade. He would be obliged to pay his owner a monthly payment representing interest on the capital invested, the rest he lived on and saved up. When he had saved sufficient to pay his ransom and repay his owner's loan, plus the city's redemption charges, he was free to return home. Some captives in this category possessed only mercantile skill. An Irishman who was held a captive at Algiers not long after the Baltimore episode described how an English captive searched the streets of Algiers for work to enable him to keep his wife and child with him. After a difficult start, this man became a prosperous merchant.

The fourth category of captives was those that were purchased as a tribute to Allah. This applied exclusively to young boys.

A number of the wealthy citizens of Algiers city would purchase young Christian boys on the market place in order to take them into their homes and have them instructed in the Moslem faith for the greater glory of Allah. Once having got over the uncomfortable hurdle of circumcision these young converts seem to have settled well into their new environment. In the same way most young Christian women who found their way into the women's quarters of Algerian households wealthy enough to own slaves seem to have settled in without much drama. Accounts at this time imply that a concubine in Algiers was seldom ill-treated and, with most of the domestic drudgery being performed by negress slaves, life was probably a good deal easier for a woman there than it had been in far West Cork. Certainly the climate was dryer and the houses sturdier and more convenient.

In the letter-book of the great Earl of Cork, preserved in the muniment room at Chatsworth House there is a six–page report on the Baltimore raid written at Dublin during the following February (1632). This letter places the blame for the attack on Baltimore firmly on the shoulders of Captain Hooke of the Fifth Whelp and Sir Thomas Button. The letter further says that despite the fact that the government has since paid out £3649.3.5. neither of the Whelps are providing much service. The Fifth Whelp's crew was still very disorderly and had slain a lieutenant and wounded several soldiers in a fracas. The Earl states that Hackett was put on trial at his command. He also claims to have heard indirectly from an escaped captive that the Turks planned another attack the following summer on a much larger scale, and that rumours of this assault were likely to frighten away the pilchard fishermen from the seas and the English planters from the coast. He estimates the fisheries brought between twenty and fifteen thousand pounds worth of French and Dutch currency into the country every year and that it might be a good investment to send more warships to defend the Irish coast. He states that the English planters of Baltimore would agree to contribute heavily towards building a fort or blockhouse if the king would give them some cannon and protect them from the demands of Sir Walter Coppinger. He implies that Sir Walter could probably be persuaded to leave the planters in peace.

"Wee may not omitt upon this occasion to make known to your lordships...what miseries those poor english captives which were taken from Baltimore doo suffer at Argeers...as by letters sent from thence may appeare...and doo herewith humbly offer them to your lpps views, Beseeching...that you will be pleased to direct some course...whereby the English Consull now Lodgied at Argeers may use his best meanes for their enlargement, Amonge many others yt suffer by yt accident there is one willm Gunter who beares ye greatest pt in that loss, having his wife and seaven sonns carried away by ye Turkes, Hee will not bee dissuaded from reparing thither to sollicite yr lpps applyinge some remedie to his greife..."

How frustrating it is that not one of these captives' letters seems to have survived the years!

By 20 June 1632 little seems to have changed at Baltimore itself. It is reasonable to suppose that some of the houses down by the Cove would have been re-thatched and refurbished; others would have been left empty and roofless to disintegrate in the moist sea breezes. Now, however, there were soldiers billeted at Dún na Séad, the town fort that Sir Walter Coppinger had been obliged to hand over to the military by the Council of Munster. There were rumours circulating that the Algerians would return this year. The Fifth Whelp had been sent away to join the Ninth at Briston for a complete re-fit. Beacons had been set up on the summits of all prominent hills along the coast. Certain reliable men had been given the task of lighting these, but only when Algerian warships had been definitely sighted making to land. Small forces of cavalry were stationed at strategic points inland ready to move quickly to any point on the coast where danger threatened.

So, somehow or other, Sir Walter had lost even the fort, Dún na Séad, which was supposed to have compensated him for being cheated out of Baltimore. Why was Sir Walter thus ill-treated? What did the English suspect about his role in the events at Baltimore? As for Hackett, he was hanged — not two years later, as some say, but very soon, as soon as possible. In 1844 an Irish nationalist poet named Thomas Davis wrote a ballad on the Sack of Baltimore in which he implied that Hackett was a traitor to Ireland:

> Tis two long years since sunk the town beneath
>   that bloody band,
> And all around its trampled hearths a larger
>   concourse stand,
> Where, high upon a gallows tree, a yelling
>   wretch is seen —
> 'Tis Hackett of Dungarvan — he who steered
>   the Algerine!
> He fell amid a sullen shout, with scarce a pass-
>   ing prayer,
> For he had slain the kith and kin of many a
>   hundred there,

Some muttered of MacMurchadh, who
    brought the Norman o'er
Some cursed him with Iscariot, that day in
    Baltimore.

The joke here is that Hackett was not a traitor to *Ireland* but to England; he was executed by the English for betraying English interests in Ireland. By modern standards Hackett was an *Irish Patriot*, and Murad Reis can be compared to those Germans recruited by Roger Casement in 1916 (who however never showed up, leaving the Easter Rising to fail on its own):—Murad was a Moorish supporter of the Irish Cause.

To summarize the rest of the story of the captives:

—No money was sent to ransom them from England, since the official position was that success would only encourage the corsairs to try again. "No negotiations with terrorists," as we might say.

—Consul James Frizell in Algiers fell on hard times. There are indications that his desperate financial position forced him to unworthy measures. An English captive writing to his wife in 1632 advised her to send his ransom money to Leghorn. He urged her at all costs not to send it to the Jewish brokers of Consul Frizell for these people had a way of holding on to ransom monies until the slave for whom it was sent had died, and after that no one ever heard of the funds again.

—By 1633 only one captive (a woman) had been redeemed, by a mysterious character named Job Frog Martino of Lugano. All the rest, according to Consul Frizell, had either died or turned Turk.

—In the list furnished by the Lords Justices and Council of Ireland to the Privy Council, which is reproduced in the Calendar of State Papers for Ireland of 10 July 1631, are numbered eleven boys; there is also listed a number of children. As all the children were unlikely to be of the same sex, it seems reasonable to assume that the term "boy" as used in this list meant male child old enough to be separated from his mother. It was "boys" of this age that were of most interest to devout Moslems and it is likely that the eleven listed would have been persuaded by the Algerians to embrace Islam. All accounts left by Christians held captive at Algiers, from that written by Cervantes in the 16th century until the last days of the Regency in the early 19th century, insist that strenuous efforts were made to convert boy captives to the Moslem faith. Most of these conversions were effected by kindness, for the Turks and renegades seemed to get pleasure out of the cheerful manners of their young converts; but there are also, distressingly, accounts of force being used when boys resisted conversion.

—Allowing for a number of conversions and a few sales to other parts of North Africa and the Levant, it still seems that a substantial number of the captives must have died during the first two and a half years of their captivity. Yet the Baltimore captives were fortunate, for the plague which was a menacing and regular visitor along the coast of North Africa, had not been recorded in Algiers since 1624. Nevertheless, smallpox, cholera, typhoid, typhus and measles took constant toll there, while some of the very young children may have soon succumbed to new strains of dysentery.

—A growing conviction that they had been forgotten by the authorities and their families at home must have persuaded many to shrug their shoulders and throw in their lot entirely with the new estate into which they had been so roughly introduced. It could well have been that the people from Baltimore, seeing how the Icelanders had settled down at Algiers, may have decided that there was something to be said for the Mediterranean coast, as opposed to the windswept shores of the North Atlantic.

—After the Revolution, Cromwell decided to ransom all the English captives in Algiers, and sent one Edmund Carson there to arrange for their release.

> The list compiled by Edmund Cason in 1645 includes only one of the people seized out of Baltimore in 1631. Her name is given as Joan Broadbrook and although she is written down in the records she still remains something of a mystery. Amongst the people named as having been taken out of Baltimore in the document sent to the Privy Council at Whitehall in July 1631 was Stephen Broadbrook, wife and two children. Joan Broadbrook, accordingly, could either have been Stephen's wife or daughter. Not one of the other Baltimore people is listed as having been redeemed by Edmund Cason. One hundred and five people had vanished without trace. One woman is recorded as having ransomed herself in 1634 but of the rest we know nothing. There is nothing in any records to show if any one of them ever returned to Baltimore.

Sometime after his return from Ireland, Murad Reis had the incredible bad luck—for once in his life—to be taken prisoner by the Knights of Malta. Our old friend Père Dan was actually present in Algiers when the news of this calamity was reported. "One day I saw in the street more than 100 women rushing pell-mell to console the wife of that renegade and corsair" [Murad Reis]; "this they accomplished, vying with one another in great demonstrations of dole and woe, not without shedding of tears, whether real or feigned, as is their custom upon such untoward and fatal occasions."

In 1640—no one knows how—Murad Reis effected his release or escape from the dreadful Knights of "the religion", and reappeared in his old haunts again. He returned to Morocco, where the Sultan was moved to appoint him governor of the fortress of Oualidia, near the coastal town of Safi, not far from the old stomping grounds of Salé. As Coindreau says, it was a sort of "golden retirement" for the aging pirate.

> On December 30th [Coindreau says the 24th] of that year a Dutch ship entered Sallee [actually Safi], where Jansz was Governor of the Castle. The ship brought a new Dutch consul who had with him, as a pleasant little surprise for the pirate, his daughter Lysbeth, now grown into an attractive young woman.
>
> The meeting moved all beholders. Jansz "was seated in great pomp on a carpet, with silk cushions, the servants all round him." When father and daughter met, "both began to cry, and having discoursed for some time he took his leave in the manner of royalty." Lysbeth afterwards went to stay with her father until the following August in his castle at Maladia, some miles inland, "but the general opinion on board was that she had already had her fill of that people and that country." In any event she returned to Holland and we hear no more about her. Presumably she married a worthy Dutchman who had nothing to do with the sea or Morocco.

How Jansz died no one knows. The only hint we have, an ominous one, is contained in the biography of him by the Schoolmaster of Oostzaan, whose concluding sentence is "His end was very bad." [Gosse, 57–8]

Naturally, as a pirate, Murad *had* to come to a "bad end." But the pious biographer here cannot even call on the plague (as with Captain Ward) to conjure up some sort of fearful and exemplary demise for Jan Jansz. For all we know he died asleep in bed—perhaps even in the good graces of Allah.

VIII

THE CORSAIR'S CALENDAR

Throughout this study we've used the words *corsair* and *pirate* as if they were synonyms, but this is really not quite correct. In the strict sense a pirate is a sea-going criminal, while a corsair operates like a *privateer* who is granted "letters of marque" or a commission by one government to attack the shipping of another. A privateer is only a criminal from the point of view of the ships he attacks; from his own point of view he's committing a legitimate act of war. In the case of the corsairs, the situation is complicated by the concept of a religious war which transcends national interests. Algiers, Tunis, and Tripoli commissioned privateers in the name of the Sublime Porte, which expected the corsairs to honor all Ottoman treaties, and not to attack ships of nations at peace with Turkey. Several times attempts were made to discipline corsairs who broke this rule; if the attempts were half-hearted and usually unsuccessful, the corsairs—by their own lights—were simply obeying a higher power, the demands of the permanent *jihad*. Brown quotes Moroccan historians to demonstrate the ideological basis of Salé's actions:

> In a chapter headed "The Fleet of the Holy War or the Slawi Piracy" (*ustul al-jihad aw al-*

qarṣana aṣ-ṣalawiya), Muhammad Hajji has pointed out that piracy, the Arabic *qarṣana*, is not to be understood in terms of the foreign derivations of its original Latin meaning, that is, the French *course*, privateering. "Rather," he writes, "I mean by the Slawi corsairs those warriors (*mujahids*), Andalous and Moroccans, who boldly embarked in their ships on the waves of the ocean to defend the territory of the homeland or to rise against the Spaniards who forced upon the Muslims of al-Andalus the worst kind of suffering and unjustly made them leave their homes and possessions."

Thus, for the people of Salé, fighting and looting on high seas or the coasts of Europe was justified as a continuation both of the holy wars of the earlier dynasties and of the defense of the coast by the likes of al-Ayyashi. The corsairs, "men of noble and proud character," had the blessings of the saints of Salé and were integrated into the community of the city. That is not to deny, however, that at least some pirates were renegades and that their original purpose in coming to Salé was to share in the general wealth brought by the "holy war." "Look in the trunk of the Hassar family and you will find an old Christian sailor's cap. The *uluj* [Christian slave] origin of the Fenish family is no more hidden than the blue of their eyes" are derisory comments still heard in Salé when people talk about some of the old renegade families of the city. Although there were *aslamis* (coll., converts to Islam) in Salé, their origins were not an obstacle to complete assim-

> ilation to the norms and values of the commu-
> nity, nor to their reaching positions of power in
> Society. The pressures toward social and cul-
> tural integration in Salé made these renegade
> pirates into warriors in the name of religion."
> [Brown, 1971: 53]

Salé-Rabat, of course, was beholden to no outside government in the first half of the 17th century, but commissioned corsairs in the name of the Republic; and the Republic
consisted—more-or-less—of the corsairs themselves.
Algiers, Tunis, and Tripoli have been called "corsair states",
but in truth only "Sallee" deserves that definition.

The easiest way to understand the difference between a
pirate and a privateer is to examine the different ways they
split up the booty. Pirate captains very frequently took only
one-and-a-half or two shares, the ship's officers took one-and-
a-half or one-and-a-fourth, the crewmen one share, and non-
combatants (boys and musicians!) one-half or three-fourths.
By contrast a privateer captain usually took 40 shares to the
crewman's single share. Of course, one share in a successful
privateering cruise could be worth far more than a salary in
the merchant marine—or unpaid impressment into a Navy—
but the contrast with piratical egalitarianism is very striking.
Pirates were very nearly communistic in their pure state.
Scholars who see them simply as proto-capitalists are making
a big mistake. Pirates don't fit the Marxist definition of "social
bandit" (i.e., "primitive revolutionary") because pirates have
no "social" context, no society of peasants for whom they
serve as focal elements of resistance. Marxists like Hobsbawm
never include the pirates among their approved "precursors"
of true radicalism because they see the pirates—at best—as
individuals involved in resistance simply as a form of self-
aggrandizement and primitive accumulation. They forget that

groups of pirates formed their own social spheres, and that the "governments" of these groups (as expressed in ships' "articles") were both anarchistic in affording maximum individual freedoms, and communistic in eliminating economic hierarchy. The social organization of the pirates has no parallel in any of the *states* of the 15–18th centuries—*except Rabat-Salé.* The Republic of Bou Regreg was not a pure pirate utopia, but it was a state founded on piratical principles; in fact, it was the *only* state ever founded on these principles.[30]

Once again, an examination of the division of spoils will give us a precise structural insight into corsair society. In the Ottoman Barbary states:

> The scale for division of the profits of a cruise is instructive. In the 1630's the pasha took 12 percent in Algiers, 10 percent in Tunis, the repairs for the mole 1 percent; the marabout, 1 percent. Of the remaining 88 or 86 percent, half went to the shipowners, and the other half to the crew and soldiers. Of the second half the reis received 10–12 parts, the agha 3 parts, the pilot 3 parts, navigator 3 parts, sail master 3 parts, master of the hatch 2 parts, surgeon 3 parts, sailors 2 parts; if there were Moors aboard, they were given only 1 part "because they are people on whom one does not count much." If any of these people were slaves, the patron took their shares and sometimes gave part of it to the slaves. Dan's account of the

30. Unless it be G. d'Annunzio's infamous Republic of Fiume (1919), which financed its brief existence by piracy, and had a constitution based on the idea of music as the only force of social organization. See Philippe Julien, trans., *D'Annunzio.*

division corresponds approximately with those of other informants. [Wolfe, 1979: 144. The Marabout is the Sufi or shrine-guardian who blesses the ships and prays for their success.]

We see that ship owners receive half the profits after "taxes", but in many cases the captains owned their own ships. Even so, this practise certainly seems proto-capitalist. On the other hand, the captain as captain (rather than as owner) receives only 10 to 12 times as much as the worst-paid crew man, while European privateer captains were paid 40 times. This seems to indicate a somewhat egalitarian approach.

The data from Salé is a bit difficult to interpret. According to Coindreau,

> the usual method of divying the spoils under the Moorish Republic was as follows:
> —10% to the central authority (the Divan of Salé);
> —half the remainder, to the outfitter [l'armateur] (or to the rais) to indemnify him for damages incurred on the expedition;
> —the other half—45% of the total booty—to the ship's crew. Officers, pilot, master gunner and surgeon usually received 3 parts, while the master of manoevers, the calfat, and the cannoneers—two parts.
> [Coindreau, p. 64]

No prey, no pay, as all pirates agreed—but even in the event of a fruitless voyage, the crew was not charged for provisions.

This doesn't tell us what the captain received if he was *not* the owner/outfitter of the ship, but rather commissioned directly by the Divan (which owned ships in its own right) or by some group of shareholders or shipowners. Assuming the captain owned and provisioned his ship, he earned 45%, more or less the same as a European privateer captain. If not, he probably made something more like the 10–12% of the Algerian captains. Captains who owned many ships could become exceedingly wealthy, as in the case of Murad Reis, the Dutch Renegado who actually rose to the leadership of the Republic.

Clearly Rabat/Salé was not organized like a pure pirate venture—but it was not organized like a European or Islamic monarchy either. The big difference between Algiers and Salé was that the "tax" off the top went to Istanbul in the first case, but in the second case, *stayed in Salé*. It was used to benefit the corsairs (repair the ramparts, finance expeditions, etc.) rather than to fatten some distant sultan. Salé's wars with the Saadians, the Marabout al-Ayyashi, and the Alewite dynasty, etc., all centered around the 10%, which was both the symbol and the cost of corsair independence. Salé was neither as anarchic nor as communistic as "Libertatia" (see below) or other real-life pirate utopias—but it was far more so than any European country. Its Governor-Admiral and its Divan were elected and could be un-elected every year if they failed to represent the people's interests. Everyone capable of shipping on a cruise stood a chance at wealth. Even "captives of war" could earn freedom and wealth as Renegadoes. As for the professional pirates who joined the Republic, once again we see that although they lost the pure autonomy of real piracy, they gained a home, a society, a source of backing, a market, and a place to *enjoy* their wealth—everything a pirate might well lack and most yearn for. It was worth taking a cut in pay to gain all that, obviously.

The mouth of the Bou Regreg river, which served Rabat-Salé as a harbor, was protected by a treacherous sand-bar which prevented enemy ships and European naval fleets with their deep keels from getting close enough to shore for an effective bombardment—but this feature also limited the corsairs in certain ways. For one thing, their vessels—even the "round ships"—had to be small and shallow-draft, which made long cruises difficult. Fleeing into port under pursuit, they might be detained by a low tide and suffer capture within sight of home, as happened on several sad occasions. But whatever the Saletin ships lacked—storage for provisions, for example, or sufficient tonnage to support much heavy cannon—they made up for in speed and maneuverability, and in the profound seamanship of their captains. Moreover, Moslem navigators were familiar with (and even invented) such scientific devices as the astrolabe, and no longer depended on dead reckoning or coast-hugging tactics. Officers and crew alike made do with very short provisions and very uncomfortable quarters. Thus the area of activity of the corsairs was greater than might be expected; the raid on Iceland was an exception, but even the English channel was unsafe (a Sallee Rover was once captured in the Thames estuary).

In the 17th century, winter was still an off–season for merchant shipping, corsairs, and even grand navies. The corsairs followed a seasonal pattern and spent at least three or four months every year at home in Salé, attending to politics or love affairs, married life or debauch, wheeling and dealing, repairing and shipbuilding—or perhaps even to the practise of Sufism—according to their wonts and wants.

Come springtime, usually in May, a corsair would look for a position with the fleet, which probably consisted (during our period) of forty or sixty small ships of the types depicted by Coindreau:

Caravelle

Tartano

Polacre

Chebec

Senau

Roughly half the fleet would head north, probably to the lucrative hunting ground off the Iberian peninsula, and the other half would turn south toward the Canaries and Azores, where they would lurk in wait for stragglers from the huge flotillas of Spain and Portugal returning from the New World with cargoes of gold. For ordinary cruising purposes two or three ships would stick together; in case a prize was captured, a vessel could be spared to escort it back to Salé while the rest kept prowling the waves. Each ship held scant provisions of *boucan*[31] and cous-cous for perhaps two months at most. If

---

31. On Hispaniola the Buccaneers were hunters who prepared boucan or smoked dried meat for ship provisions.

ships needed to re-provision or repair, they might call in at any of several Moroccan coastal towns (at least during periods when these were not held by European powers) such as Tetouan, Mamora, Fedala, Azemmour, or Safi. Sometimes some of the fleet headed through the Straits of Gibraltar and raided the shipping and even the coasts of Mediterranean Spain and France—but this was usually considered the proper stomping grounds of Algiers, Tunis, and Tripoli. But the other Barbary state corsairs seldom if ever made it as far into the Atlantic as the Sallee Rovers. In 1625 they carried off captives from Plymouth in England; in 1626 five ships were seized off the coast of Wales; in 1627 they reached Iceland and sacked the city of Reykjavik, where the booty was scant but the blond captives no doubt proved popular in the slave markets. A great deal of activity centered in the waters between England and Ireland, and we assume that the corsairs used some of the remote lawless smugglers' ports of Southern and Western Ireland as friendly harbours. In the Newfoundland banks the Saletin fleet captured more than 40 fishing vessels in the space of two years, and in 1624 a dozen or so ships from Salé appeared on the coasts off Acadia or Nova Scotia. When the English fleet came to Salé in 1637, the purpose was to ransom poor fishermen from English vessels seized off Newfoundland.

One musn't imagine the typical Sallee Rover—or indeed any sensible pirate—as lusting for violence, or even as particularly cruel. The Comte de Castries put it thus: "Rather than chance the glory of combat they preferred their prey disarmed and peaceful." [Quoted by Coindreau, 1948: 133] It's an historian's cliché to say that the 17th century was "cruel", or indeed that *any* century prior to the 19th or 20th was "cruel". Once the modernist Euro-American chauvinism is stripped from such remarks, we are left with a *perceived difference* between "then" and "now". The modern era has succeeded in repressing consciousness of its own cruelty by mediating between the act and the perception of the act, by means of technology. We call up and revel in *images* of violence in ways that would seem utterly diabolical to the meanest thug in the Bou Regreg Republic, and we create death and destruction in precisely the same disembodied and alienated fashion: by pushing a button. In the 17th century, despite advances in artillery, most life-and-death struggles had to be decided in hand-to-hand combat, using a technology not much advanced over that of the Bronze Age. (In fact, one credulous European traveller, William Lemprière, was persuaded by a humorous "native informant" in Salé that the corsairs' chief tactic was to hurl *rocks* at other ships — and this seemed quite reasonable to him, if a trifle primitive.) [Lemprière, 1791] A few pirates, like Low and Blackbeard, appear to have been sea-going sadists in a very precise and clinical sense of the term, and no doubt Salé attracted a few such types. But the truth is that combat is *dangerous*, and it's *hard work*. Corsairs were interested in booty, not "glory" (as a Frenchman might assume) or "manliness" (as an Englishman might assume); they were happy to be considered "cowards and bullies" so long as they *won*. And therefore they resorted to trickery and camouflage first, and only whipped out their flintlocks and scimitars as a last resort. Piracy can be viewed as an extreme case of the zerowork mentality: five or six months lolling around the Moorish cafés, then a summer cruise on a nice blue ocean, a few hours of exertion, and hey presto, another year of idleness has been financed. If pirates weren't lazy, they'd be cobblers or lead miners or fishermen — but like gangsters in old movies they thought "work is for saps," and used every expedient to avoid it. As Père Dan said, "The corsairs give chase to no Christain merchants without believing themselves the stronger; for if it be not the case that they enjoy an advantage of several to few, or of a great fleet to a small one, they rarely attack — for it's true that these infamous pirates are dastardly cowards at heart and never give battle without possessing great advantage." [Coindreau, 1948: 134]

Naturally every corsair vessel would carry a fine collection of the flags and pennants of all nations, and would first attempt to pass as English to an English ship or Spanish to a Spanish; their own flag, the Man in the Moon, was doubtless rarely seen.[32] The trick of switching flags with Algerian corsairs has already been described.

Henry Mainwaring, in his memoirs, relates that the Sallee Rovers would strike all their sails at dawn and send a look-out aloft to scan the horizons for possible prey — once sighted, the potential victim would be scrutinized at length and discussed: merchantman or naval vessel? Too big to tackle or too small to bother? What strategy to adopt, what flag to unfurl, etc.? [Quoted in Coindreau, 1948: 137]

Having decided on pursuit and action, the corsairs would hope that a few cannon shots would induce a rational mood in the enemy captain (especially if his ship was insured!), and an immediate surrender. If not, they would have to board. "It is a terrible thing," says Père Dan, "to behold with what fury they attack a vessel. They swarm aboard the poopdeck, sleeves rolled to elbows and scimitars in hand, all together making a great hullabaloo to wither the courage of their victims." Hopefully the show of menace and

_____

32. The flag of Salé, using an Islamic crescent but adding the image of a human face, seems to symbolize the Renegado's creed with heraldic precision. One is reminded of the legend that the Templars worshipped the Head of Baphomet and that the Moor's Head is a symbol in Rosicrucian alchemy; it's interesting to note that some modern Christian Fundamentalists consider the Man in the Moon a satanic device.

the wild shrieking would do the trick — real combat was the last resort and least favored tactic of all.

Whether or not a ship carried specie or cargo of any value, its crew and passengers constituted a guaranteed source of income.[33] In Islamic Law "Captives of (holy) war" were not considered in the same category as "slaves", but in some ways their position was worse. Slaves had distinct rights in Law, after all, but captives were simply human booty. That Salé financed its freedom by the ransoming and sale of human beings naturally tarnishes that freedom in our eyes, but we should hesitate to apply our modern sentiments to Salé alone. The Knights of Malta practised the same economics, but enjoyed no proto-democratic freedoms — and the British Navy "impressed" unwilling recruits into virtual slavery. In any case, since Moroccan sailors had given up the use of oar-driven galleys, few of their captives would suffer the fate of thousands upon thousands (like Miguel de Cervantes, or the early American anarchist William Harris of Rhode Island) [See Wilson, 1993] who languished as "galley slaves" in Algerian ships — or for that matter, in Maltese or Spanish ships.

---

33. "From 1618 to 1626 alone, 6,000 Christians were captured and ransomed and prizes taken to the value of more than fifteen million pounds. In ten years, 1629–39, the Morisco Customs registered a total of 25 or 26 million ducats." [Caillé, 1949: 224] In 1626 a petition was presented to the Duke of Buckingham by "the distress'd wives of almost 2,000 poor mariners remaining most miserable captives in Sallee in Barbary." These poor husbands are "suffering such unspeakable misery and tortures that they are almost forc'd to convert from their Christian religion." [Norris, 1990: 66] The price of saving 2,000 souls from turning Turke might well be too high even for a Duke.

He that's condemn'd to th'oare hath first his face,
Eyebrowes and head close shaven (for more disgrace
cannot betide a Christian). Then, being stript
to th' girdle (as when roagues are to be whipt),
Chain'd are they to the seates where they sit rowing,
Five in a row together; a Turke going
on a large plancke between them, and though their eyes
are ready to starte out with pulling, he cryes
"Worke, worke you Christian curres," and though
    none needs
one blow for loytering, yet his bare back bleeds
and riseth up in bunches.
— from "The Lamentable Cries of Prisoners in Algiers
    under the Turkes" (1624) [in Norris, 1990: 66]

Defoe describes Robinson Crusoe's life as a Sallee captive in more realistic terms than the fund-raising fanatics who toured Europe edifying audiences with tales of exotic tortures and rapes, and who were frequently suspected — even then — of "yellow journalism". Salé had no vast agricultural lands upon which to use their slaves, as in America, nor any industries in which to employ unskilled forced labor. The captives were primarily *merchandise*, and as always with merchandise the rule was, you break it, you buy it. No one pays ransom for a corpse.

Thus the corsair's first task, which began immediately after taking a prize, was to determine the identities, or at least the qualities, of their captives. Renegadoes who spoke their languages would interrogate them, using guile by preference to torture, to elicit details. The corsairs developed a fascination with *hands*: soft hands of an aristo or merchant, calloused hands of a mere mariner, peculiar signs and deformations of certain trades and crafts, the telltale inkstain of literacy, even the lines of chiromancy to determine health, fate, personality.

Certain captives, too poor for ransom but possessed of valuable skills, would be offered freedom if they turned Turk—armorers, metallurgists, shipbuilders, and the like were highly prized, and a literate man might aspire to the rank of seagoing scribe (one for each crew, to read captive ships' manifests and logs), or even a clerk's job in the Divan, or with some merchant or consul.

A young Irishman from Galway named Richard Joyce (or Joyes), emigrating to the West Indies in 1675, was captured by Algerian corsairs and held captive in Algiers for 14 years. There upon his arrival

> he was purchased by a wealthy Turk who followed the profession of a goldsmith, and who observing his slave...to be tractable and ingenious, instructed him in his trade in which he speedily became an adept. The Moor, as soon as he heard of his release [i.e., that Joyce had been ransomed], offered him, in case he should remain, his only daughter in marriage, and with her half his property, but all these, with other tempting and advantageous proposals, Joyce resolutely declined; on his return to Galway he married, and followed the business of a goldsmith with considerable success, and, having acquired a handsome independence, he was enabled to purchase the estate of Rahoon...from Colonel Whaley, one of Cromwell's old officers. [Quoted from J. Hardiman, 1820.]

The secret of Joyce's success, according to Galway legend, was a ring he designed in Algiers based on Moorish symbols, a crowned heart (sometimes with a rose) held by two hands—the famous Claddagh Ring, symbol of love and friendship, almost as "Irish" as the Shamrock.

Joyce was not the only Barbary captive who ended by owing his fortune to some trade practiced or even learned in captivity.[34]

One of the rare first-hand accounts of Salé was written by a French captive, Germaine Mouette, "captured at sea December 16, 1670, sold at Salé on All Saints Day, for the sum of 360 *écus*."

> His owners numbered four, of whom one actually held him as a slave. The other three each owned one-sixth of Mouette, having gone right away to the fondouk [or *bagno*, slave quarters] where he was taken after his sale [i.e., the other three bought sub-shares from the first owner]. The oldest was Muhammad al-Marrakchi, a government official, the second was a merchant of wool and oil called Mohammad Liebus, and the third was a Jew, Rabbi Yamin. M. al-Marrakchi took the slave home with him, where his wife gave Mouette white bread and butter with honey, and a few dates and raisins of Damascus. He was then returned to the fondouk, where he received a

---

34. For this and other fascinating legends (e.g. the first Claddagh ring was dropped in the lap of a young girl by an eagle!), see the delightful amateur history by Richard Joyce's descendant Cecily Joyce, *Claddagh Ring Story*, 1990.

visit from the Jew who greeted him ceremoniously and promised him his freedom if his family would pay the ransom demanded by the four owners. If he did not at once write a letter to France to ask for this sum, he would be beaten with sticks and left to die in a pit. Mouette at once complied, but decided to lie and pretend to be no more than the brother of a cobbler—so the renegado who was serving as translator for the Jew declared that no profit could be expected in the sale of this slave. Next day Mouette was sent to the third owner, the wool and oil merchant, whose wife and mother-in-law took pity on the captive. At first they put him to grinding wheat, but when that task proved too tiring, they made him companion to the merchant's little son. When the good wife saw that the boy had grown attached to Mouette, she regaled him with more bread and butter, honey and fruits, and had removed from his legs the 25-pound chain he'd been forced to wear. She begged him to turn renegade and marry her niece." [Mouette managed to weasel out of this situation by showering the woman with "the most tender and touching words in the world," ending up more in favor than before.]

Mouette remained there for a year without suffering too much, thanks to his supposed poverty. But at last the fourth owner, now Governor of the Casbah, grew impatient. He claimed his rights in Mouette and took him off to work in his stable. The slave was now reduced to black bread, and shared cramped and noisome quarters with other captives and poor Arabs. The governor renewed his demands for a ransom of 1,000 *écus*, but Mouette still insisted on his poverty, and so now was sent to work with masons who were repairing the castle ramparts. The other workers mistreated him and beat him cruelly—thus finally inspiring him to raise the ransom money—and at last regain his freedom. [Penz, 1944: 13–14]

Compared with the horrendous tales of captivity circulated by Redemptionist Friars and other propagandists, Sieur Mouette's story has the ring of authenticity: clearly the captive's fate was no picnic, but it had its ups and downs, and even its possible routes of salvation or escape. Thus such accounts as the legend of Richard Joyce seem credible; and thus also we may understand how *seductive* the possibility of conversion to Islam might appear to captives like Joyce and Mouette. Those Moorish "nieces" for one thing! Those oriental women with their (almost) irresistable love magic!

Whether successful "on the account" or not, by late October every Sally Rover was back in port, the ships in a canal (between Old Salé's walls and the river, and well-protected), the Corsairs in their winter quarters, ranging in splendor no doubt from suburban palaces to squalid rented rooms off the rue des Consuls in the brawling Morisco quarters of Rabat. As for the town itself, anyone who has visited Morocco can easily picture it, since the 17th century fabric of urban space (or for that matter, the 10th century) still survives in all the old towns and even cities. Salé, unlike Rabat, has resisted modernization, and still presents the same basic pattern of narrow winding alleyways between windowless walls, bazaars, mosques, bathhouses, shadowy tea-houses, public fountains in blue and white tile—all traffic consisting of pedestrians and donkeys—smelling of spices, firewood, and sewage—and cut with the cool salt wind off the ocean.

Rabat, or "New Salé", was built largely by the Andalusian Moriscos, and made use of a grid-plan for streets quite unlike the meandering alleyways of other Moroccan cities. Domestic architecture showed Andalusian influence. The city existed on more than one level, with mysterious underground tunnels cut out beneath the surface, some of them radiating from the "Pirates' Tower," or passing beneath the famous old "Moorish Café", or the "Devil's Stairway." The city was enclosed by defensive walls, and the Casbah looming over all resembled nothing so much as a medieval castle—which, in effect, is precisely what it was.

The Moorish house remains unchanged and is still being built today in Spain and North Africa (by anyone sensible enough or poor enough to prefer traditional vernacular to concrete and sheet metal), and the model was transported even to Mexico and California—the same adobe and white-wash, the same heavy ornamented wooden doors and carved shutters, the same thick walls enclosing a 2- or 3-story square of rooms which open on an inner garden, with fruit trees, shade trees and cypresses, roses, herbs, a tiled fountain, per-haps a pavilion piled with carpets and cushions, where one might dine al fresco or smoke a waterpipe with one's coffee or mint tea. A pirate who "married the niece" or struck it rich on the *corso* might well enjoy such a house, and perhaps bach-elor sailors with means might club together to rent one. In 1630, Murad Reis and other notables of the realm welcomed a French diplomatic embassy and received them in the Casbah in a room "furnished only with carpets," where they sat or reclined on bolsters or "hassocks of red *damas;*" "a secretary took notes at a table no higher than his elbow." Thus typical Moorish decor was described by the embassy's scribe, a Capuchin Father. In 1642 other French religious, on a captive-rescuing mission, were received by "Prince" Abdullah, who gave audience "seated on a sheepskin between two trestles covered with a lean-to of fir-wood: this was his throne and dais." [*ibid*. 235][35]

---

35. Islamic simplicity must have appeared to unappreciative and baroque-minded Europeans as a kind of poverty. Our acquaintance, the Scots traveller William Lithgow, describes the costumes worn in Fez at this period, adding a few spicy observations:

The people of both kinds are cloathed in long breeches and bare ancles, with red or yellow shooes shod with iron on the heeles, and on the toes with white horne; and wear on their bodies long robes of linning or rimmery, and silken wastcoates of divers colours; the behaviour of the vulgars being far more civill toward strangers then at Constantinople or elsewhere in all Turkey.

The women here go unmasked abroad, wearing on their heads broad and round capes, made of straw or small reedes, to shade their faces from the sunne; and damnable libidinous, being prepared both wayes to satisfie the lust of their luxurious villaines; neither are they so strictly kept as the Turkish women, marching where they please.

There are some twelve thousand allowed brothel-houses in this town, the curtezans, being neatly kept, and weekely well looked to by physicians; but, worst of all, in the summer time, they openly lycenciate three thousand common stewes of sodomiticall boyes. Nay, I have seene at mitday, in the very market places, the Moores buggering these filthy carrions, and without shame or punishment go freely away.

The citizens here are very modest and zealous at their divine service, but great dancers and revellers in their solemne festivall dayes, wherein they have bul-baiting, maskerats, singing of rimes and processions of priests.

Here in Fez there bee a great number of poets, that make songs on divers subjects, especially on love and lovers, who they

In winter, the corsair's diet would improve over his shipboard rations, with spiced tajines of meat and fruit served on couscous or rice, wheatbread with butter and honey, milk and yoghurt, chicken pies with sugar and gum arabic, whole roast lambs stuffed with dates and saffron rice, gooey sweets and sugary mint tea. For the lax of faith there were fine canary wines and opportos, madeiras, sherries, sack and eau de vie—the corsairs saved all the best vintages for themselves, or so it was said.

If the Renegados enjoyed themselves, the same can perhaps not be said of certain other inhabitants of Rabat's expatriate quarter, the merchant-consuls of the various more-or-less friendly European powers. It's hard to understand why some of these Graham Greene-type consuls stayed on, year after year, in a place so obviously alien to all their values. Gaspard de Rastin, a French vice-consul whose house was looted in 1637 by a mob while he languished in prison (having been arrested for overzealousness in the case of some

---

openly name in their rimes, without rebuke or shame; all which poets, once every yeare, against Mahomets birthday, make rimes to his praise. Meanewhile in the afternoone of that festival day, the whole poets assembling in the marketplace, there is a decked chayre prepared for them, whereon they mount, one after another, to recite their verses in audience of all the people; and who by them is judged to be best, is esteemed all the yeare above the rest having this epithet "the Prince of Poets", and is by the Vicegerent and towne rewarded.

Indeede a worthy observation; and would to God it were now the custome of our Europian princes to doe the like, and especially of this Isle; then would bravest wits and quickest braines studdy and strive to show the exquisite ingeniosity of their best stiles and pregnant invention, which now is eclipsed and smothered downe, because, nowadayes, their is neither regard nor reward for such excellent pen-men.

[Quoted in *Sources Inédites*, 1935: 494–498]

French captives) never received any compensation either from Salé or France and eventually, "seeing there was nothing to be gained from Court than vain hopes, he died of sheer disappointment in 1643." [Caillé, 1949: 238] A Dutch consul, David deVries, suffered much worse and yet kept coming back. He first arrived in Salé from Brazil as a captive in 1650, and was ransomed for a stupendous amount. In 1651 he was back again in Rabat as consul, and this time was welcomed ceremoniously by the Dila'iyya Sufis who were then ruling the city. But deVries soon began to fulfil his role as the "worst treated of all the European consuls." [*ibid.*, p. 240] Angry over the seizure of a Saletine ship by Holland, a mob surrounded his house, chanting "Death to the consul! Kill him!" The French historian Caillé notes that this sort of mob action can be interpreted as evidence of a "public life…and the role of the people in the politics…of a democratic and republican form of government." [*ibid*, p. 250] In 1654 deVries was again assaulted, tossed down his own staircase, and dragged off to the *Matamore*, a silo-shaped prison, while his house was thoroughly sacked. After four nights in the noisome hole he was released but "guarded" by four Moors who, moreover, demanded to be paid a "salary" of 30 rials a night! "Here there is neither order nor justice," he complained; and in another letter home he moaned that life was hard "in this barbarous land, where one can find no amusement at all." [*ibid.*, p. 237] And yet deVries stayed on and on, and died still on the job in 1662.

Most European visitors hated Salé: "an habitation for villaines, a den for theeves, a receptacle for pirats, a rendezvouze for renegodoes, a slaughter-house of barbarous cruelty and savage barbarisme, a bane and confusion to shipping-merchants and merchandise, and a miserable dolefull dungeon for poore captived Christians" [*Sources inédites*, 1935: 376.] But for various odd reasons, some Europeans actually liked Salé.

One of the best accounts of the Corsair Republic was written by an English "Agent 007" type named John Harrison, a precursor of later romantic Islamophile spies like Sir Richard Burton, T. E. Lawrence, or Gertrude Bell. Thanks to Harrison, England was the first European nation to enter diplomatic relations with the Bou Regreg Republic. In 1627 Harrison's contacts in "Sallie" fed him an enticing bit of information — or disinformation:

> The Moriscoes also now governing at Sallie sent unto me that if I would come there to treat with them, they would shake off Mully Sidans tyrannous government, which hath bin the cause of captivating so manie of Your Majesties subjectes with the losse of their ships, goods and lives, and put themselves wholly under Your Majesties protection, as your owne subjectes. So, to doe your Majesties service, I undertook a most desperate journey by land from Tetuan to Sallie in a disguized Morish habite (the countrie being so daungerous to travayle in for straungers, all in rebueltas, acknowledging no king), for that I understood the Spaniards had laid waite to betraie me by the Alerbies, who will sell their fathers for money; so travayling over the high mountaines and hills within a little of Fez, to avoide these daungers, and the greatest parte on foote, bare-legged and pilgrime-like, yet notwithstanding, comming to the playnes and our way lying by Alcazer, there was knowne and in great daunger to have been betraied, valued at a thousand ducats, to be carried to Mamora or Allerach. But it pleased God I met with two honest Morabites or Saintes, who are of great respect in that countrie (whereof one came to see me now at Sallie, the Saint of Mismooda), and

two honest Sheaqukes, who also command over their castes or tribes, and these conveyghed me from one to another, parte by day, parte by night, cleare of all daunger, till I came to Old Sallie to the great Saint Siddie Hamet Lniashi, who ruleth over all: who all offered their services to Your Majestie for the taking of Mamora, Allerach, or any other place the Spaniards hold on the coast of Barbarie, wishing them rather in Your Majesties hands, in respect of that former friendship, trade and commerce, which hath been ever of old betuixt the English and the Moores. [*Sources Inèdites*, pp. 31–2]

After this adventure, Harrison meets Jan Janz (Murat Reis), who gives him a handful of English captives as a goodwill offering.

Harrison then returns to England to rescue a number of Moorish captives from slavery in Europe (reminding the King in his secret report that slavery is condemned by the law of God, referring His Majesty to Exodus 21!), and returns to Salé with eight of them. When he arrived,

The Captaines of the Castle sent one of their great boates with order for my landing, which I did, tho the barre somewhat fowle. Well entertayned by them and of all the Andaluzes, accomodated both with house, provisions, and all other necessaries, both for mysellff and companie, at their chardges. And an Alkaid with fyve other Andaluzes appointed to guard me for feare of any treacherie or plot of Mully Sidan, who before had sent one of his cheiffest Alkaids thither, a Spanish renegado named Agib, upon an other pretext to recover the debts due to the former Alkaid, but indeed, as after they discovered, to negociat underhand with the Moores and Lerbies adjoyning to surpriz the Castle, which not prevayling, after I was landed and the ordinance and other provisions, not without great daunger and difficultie by reason of that fowle barre, Mully Sidan writ a peremptorie letter to the Captaines of the Castle, chardging them upon their alleadgance to send me unto him. They answeared I came in peace and upon honourable tearmes from Your Majestie to redeeme your subjects captives and to treate of peace, and therefore they would entertayne me accordinglie, stay as long as I pleased, and when I pleased I should depart in peace and with an honourable dispatch. Thereupon, immediatlie dispatched his Alkaid awaie, who not far from the towne was robbed and slayne by the Lerbies, and so himsellff betraied as he meant to have betraied others. And within a day or two after, all the cavalleroes of the towne, a hundredth of the cheiffest and better sort, tooke me a hunting the wild boare, giving me verie great respect, and so from tyme to tyme have found at their hands, expressing more and more a generall affection to Your Majesty, and not only in words but in deeds, immediatlie thereupon releassing all Your Majesties subjects, according to their former promises. [*ibid.*, pp. 39–40]

With such pleasant entertainment, no wonder Harrison became enthusiastic about his new friends, the Andalusian Moriscoes of Salé. He pleads their cause with the English King, comparing their plight (mass banishment from Spain) with that of the Biblical Diaspora, or the Trojans after the fall of Troy.

Although now no face at all of Christian religion amongst them, that image of God defaced by Mahometisme, death to professe Christianity, yet manie have to me: the greater parte so distracted between that idolatrous Roman religion wherein they were borne and Mahometisme under which now they groane, as they know not what to beleive, but a verie great affection and inclination to our nation and religion, yea, even in the Moores themselves, manie of them, which without doubt is the worke of God who ruleth the hearts of all men. [*ibid.*, p. 42]

Harrison is especially taken with al-Ayyashi, the Sufi "saint" of Salé:

And twyse I went over to him, both tymes happened a shower of raine as I was with him, observed by some of the Moores as a good signe that I brought them good luck, the dew of heaven much desired in that hot and dry countrie; taking me the verie first tyme into his sell or place of devotion, where never Christian was before, for ordinarily these Saints they will not suffer any Christian to come within their doores, accounting their sanctiuaries prophaned thereby. [*ibid.*, p. 44]

According to Harrison, the new régime in Salé desires full cooperation with England in effecting the release of captives:

They have released all Your Majesties subjectes bought and sold for slaves under Mully Sidans governement and paied great sommes of money to their patrons, yea, which is more, upon this treatie they have set free a number of boyes forced to turne Moores, the most circumcised and some more who turned of infirmitie, and of their owne accordes they have promised lykewise shall be sent awaie, but by stealth, for feare of the Moores who alreadie begin to take exception and for that cause beare them the more splene, saying they be Christians in heart, all these Andaluzes, and no true Moores. And are not these uppon such tearmes worthie to be treated withall as well as Argier, which never yet, that ever I hard of, or any other place under the Turkish government, would yeeld to such tearmes, to releasse Christians once circumcised and turned Turks, but burne them (that is their law) if they recant; some of the cheefest of them taking me aside and telling me in playne tearmes they durst not doe as they could doe, but must doe things by degrees, poco a poco.

[*ibid.*, pp. 52-53]

Harrison—that British Sinbad—made seven voyages to Salé, and sad to relate, ran himself deeply into debt in pursuit of his dream—the conversion of the Moriscoes to Protestantism and full alliance with England. Not only was he disappointed, he ended suing the English government for unpaid back salary. Having failed in this, he nevertheless undertook his seventh and last voyage. Obviously he'd been bitten by the bug of obsession.

During his last long stay in Salé, Harrison involved himself deeply with local politics—in fact, he arrived in time for the Hornachero/Morisco feuding of 1629:

Coming to Salley, where we arryved the 29, I founde all in rebueltas. The Castle and the Raval or towne in cyvill dissencions one against the other. The Castle possessed and reedified by the

168

Hornacheros not long after their banishment out of Spayne, and the towne by the Andaluzes (comonly called Moriscoes), thereafter flocking thither from all partes, both of Turky and Barbary, where, after that their banishment, they were scattered like the Jewes. The Andaluzars of the towne being mo in nomber, challendging an equall share and parte with them of the Castle, bothe in the governement, customes, and other profittes and priviledges, alledgeing that they of the Castle sent for them to come there to inhabite, and that since they have borne a proporcionable parte with them in all publique charges whatsoever, demaunding 50 of the chief of the Castle to come and live with them in the towne, and 50 of the towne to goe up to the Castle, and to have an Alcaid or Governor of their owne in the towne, which they of the Castle, being the first possessors and reedifiers therof, wolde not yelde unto, but thought to bring the towne altogether into subjeccion and to their owne bowe, having all the great ordenaunce wherwith they contynually plaid into the towne, but without any great hurte, the houses being but mudd-walls, lyme and earthe. The shott onely piercing through without any battery. And they of the towne having but onely one small peece, which allso did litle hurt, to shoote att the boates passing to and againe from the Castle to the olde towne (Olde Salley) on the other side the water, which the Castle had to frinde for supply of victualls and trade, whither they had sent before all their horses and besides entertained a nomber of their horsemen in paie, which often sallied over at a forde up the river, and offended the towne, takeing their cattle and other provisions from them. And in this state, as before, I founde them in rebueltaes and cyvill warres, as they had ben not long before, but now renewed againe.

Advertisement given of my arrivall with your Majesties letteres, both the Castle and the towne seemed to be verie glad, and so expressed themselves, the Castle in discharging their best ordenaunce upon my landing, and the towne in not shooting att all for feare of hurting me or my company, which otherwise they used to doe at all boates. The Governors and chief of the Castle coming downe to the waterside to receive me and after conveying me to their Duana, where allso they receyved Your Majesties letteres with verie great respect, and thereafter againe conveyed me to my lodgeing well furnished and provided, and my diett allso and all other charges defrayed during the time of my being there. In the meane time arryved 3 of the States shippes with the Comissioners before mencioned, who presentlie came ashore, bringing with them an Agent sent from Salley before to the States; where, having stayed some five daies, they returned ashipborde, and so for Saffia.

Landed here betwixt 2 enemies, and yet both frindes and welwillers to Your Majestie and subjectes, it came into my minde (partlie desired by some of the chiefe, both of the Castle and the towne, favourers of the publique peace, and all in generall weary of the civille warres) to write a lettere to the great Saint Sydie Hamet Lyashi to move him (as all theis Sainctes professe themselves peace-makers) to come to make peace; but being then farr distant before Tanger, in the Streigths of Gibraltar, in his almahalla against the Spaniards, to whome he is a

170

mortall enemye and ever in accion and no greate frinde to Salley neither, before an answere came from him, arrived Captaine John [Murad Reis] from Tunys, Admirall of Salley, bringing with him another Sainct, the Sainct of Shelley, nere adjoyning to Sallye, who had ben at Mecha in pilgrimage to visite Mahomets tombe, and divers other Mores with him, by whose mediacion, after his new arrivall and so seasonablie, upon their Pasqua of Romedan, presentlie a peace was concluded. Agreed that the towne should have an Alcaid of their owne choise, but to be resident still in the Castle, as allso to make choise of 8 persons more to be added to those 8 of the Castle to make up their Duana or Connsell of State, in all 16, 8 for the towne and 8 for the Castle, but both these and the Alcaids to holde their sitting in the Castle, and to participate all alike, bothe in governement and all other priviledges, as one body politique. This in effect was that Sainctes order. Wherunto bothe parties had beforehand promised to stand, which, if either partie breake, he thretneth to become their utter enemye and bring in upon them the Lalbees, or countrey people, to spoyle them, as he maie easely doe, being so nere adjoyning, and they but onely watching the oportunitie of theis cyvill dissencions to be renewed againe, wherby farr greater States have ben ruyned and maie be, for trueth itself hath said it: "a kingdome or citye devided against itselfe cannot stande," as I told them of Salley, and I hope they will make use of it.

[*ibid.*, pp. 105–6]

Harrison whiles away his time in Salé negotiating for French and British interests, and quarreling with other

European adventurers (whom he accuses of irreligion). He continues to worry about the Renegado problem:

> But the feare is some maie abuse their comissions and turne pirattes, and Englishmen goe out to sea in their shippes, the shippes of Sallye, and serve under them and turne renegadors; so His Majestie looseth subjectes and God so many soules, which allso I submitt to further consideracion to be restreyned by some severe proclamacion, yea, rather to be wished (thoughe I have ben ymploied and in that respect maie seme a frinde to Sallye, yet, "magis amica patria" the honour of my countrey and generall good of Christendome is neerer and deerer to me), I saie, thoughe I have ben a meanes of that treutie of peace thereby to redeme Your Majesties subjectes oute of captivitie (as I have ben this time allso for the Frenche), yet nowe that, both the one and the other, all the English and French captives are cleared from thence, I could wishe, I saie, Your Majestie and brother of Fraunce wolde joyne yor forces for the suppressing of all the shippes belonging to that place, and Argier likewise, to prevent both theis and other inconveniences or rather indignities, Lastima! a pitifull case, so many Christians daylie taken by their shippes and made slaves, yea, a greate nomber forced to forsake their faithe, turne Turkes and renegadors, which maie easelie be remedied, if it please Your Majestie to take into consideracion the motives hereunto annexed. [*ibid.*, p. 114]

In his final report, composed in 1631, Harrison has lost a bit of his earlier enthusiasm for "Saints":

Within a year or two after arose out of the Sahara, or deserts towardes Guinie, a levantado or rebell, one of their morabittes or saintes (as they call them), who for the most part are negromancers, yet pretending great holines and austeritie of lyfe, fasting some of them everie day throughout the whole yeare, yet all the night, so long as they can see a star, may both eate and drinck: and so all the Moores are bound by their law, once everie yeare, to observe their Romedan, in nature of our Lent, for a whole moone togither but the preciser sort of these saintes doe it for a whole yeare, yea, from yeare to yeare during their lives, by which meanes (as the Popish clergie) they get to themselves a great opinion among the simple people and are reverenced as pettie Popes or rather demy-gods, thinking they know all things and can doe all things what they please; and by that reason also stand in great awe of them. Especiallie this Saint, above all the rest (called by a nickname Bumhalli, his right name Hamet), abused most the credulitie of the simple people, pretending and making them believe he was sent of God to reforme the whole countrie misgoverned by Muley Sidan. [*ibid.*, p. 141]

But even now Harrison has not lost all his romantic notions. He's still trying to persuade the King that the Moriscos are ripe for conversion to Christianity or Englishism or both:

Especiallie the Moriscoes overjoyed, grounding upon an old prophecie which they told me their auncestors found written instead in Monte Santo, neere Granada, fortelling that their banishment out of Spaine into Barbarie, but that in tyme they should be brought backe againe, and that in Christian ships; which tyme, hearing of this so great a preparation of our English fleet, they thought veriely was now comme for the finall accomplishment of that prophecie, and thereupon provided themselves of biskett, pieces, powder and all other necessaries, ready to march, expecting only the arrivall of that great Armada (as they tearmed it) to transport them. But that great designe not taking effect answeareable to so great an expectation, that faire opportunitie was lost; the Spaniardes, before trembling, now triumphing, saying to the Moores (as they related to me) there were no moe Drakes in England, all were hens, gallinas. And in the meantyme Sir Albertus Morton dead, I was likewise dead and forgotten, left there forlorne and destitute either of ship or other meanes promised to be sent unto me to transport me from thence. So was forced to take a desperat journey by land from Tetuan to Sallie, in great daunger both of my lyfe and libertie, the Spaniardes on that coast having intelligence of that my imployment and journey, having laid wait among the barbarous people to betray me, who for money will sell their own fathers and children, and have don, as I was informed: a thousand ducates offered (as I had intelligence) to bring me into Allarach or anie other of their garisons.

[*ibid.*, pp. 145-6]

A Lawrence of Arabia before his time, Harrison ends by "engaging mysellff to have tenn thousand of these Moriscoes ready to serve His Majesty"!

As for the corsairs' notorious bad behaviour—drunkery, whoring, carousing, and rioting—obviously not even the rowdiest rogue could keep it up full-time from autumn till spring. Little by little the Europeans and especially the Renegadoes would fall into Moorish rhythms of life—a daily routine, whether work or socializing in cafés, punctuated by weddings, funerals, circumcisions, festivals, public performances by dervish orders, and of course the occasional outbreak of feuding between Salé and Rabat. A Renegado might begin to take an interest in religion out of ennui if nothing else—after all, the local culture was thoroughly commingled with and permeated by spirituality, and it must have been hard to avoid. If our Renegado had learned some Arabic, or married into a Spanish-speaking Morisco family, he might learn quite a lot simply by watching and listening. Some, perhaps, might go so far as to get involved on some level.

Such prominent public figures as al-Ayyashi or M. al-Hajj of the Dala'iyya represented a highly orthodox and yet profoundly mystical aspect of Islam, which we might call classical urban-literate North African Sufism. The theosophy and even gnosis of such important writers as the 13th-century Andalusian Sufi Ibn 'Arabi were contained within a structure of strict Sunni orthopraxis and austere piety and ascesis. The orders were organized very precisely and with strict gradings of rank, from the all-powerful charismatic shaykh or *murshid* (comparable to the Hindu *guru*), to the lowest and most obedient disciple or *murid*. Meditation, retreat, invocation and recital of litanies in the *majalis* or meetings of the Order, made up the spiritual practice added to the ordinary religious practice of prayer, fasting, almsgiving, etc. The tremendous prestige of certain shaykhs could manifest itself as political power. It seems highly unlikely that any of these Orders would have appealed to or been willing to admit a Renegado, but it's not impossible. In fact, a fascinating document purporting to give an account of the captivity of St. Vincent de Paul, hints that an educated captive and an educated Moor might well share a fascination with mysticism. Unfortunately recent scholarship has cast this text into the realm of pseudepigrapha; but luckily Gosse, in his stylish and entertaining *History of the Pirates*, still believed in the text's authenticity and quoted the whole thing. It may not be true, but it's extremely important because it was *believed* to be true—because it was *believable*. (This same argument will be made for Defoe's perhaps apocryphal account of Captain Mission's Libertatia.) Here is the relevant passage:

> I was sold to a fisherman, and by him to an aged alchemist, a man of great gentleness and humility. This last told me he had devoted fifty years to a search for the Philosopher's Stone. My duty was to keep up the heat of ten or twelve furnaces, in which office, thank God, I found more pleasure than pain. My master had great love for me, and liked to discourse of alchemy and still more of his creed, towards which he did his best to draw me, with the promise of wealth and all the secrets of his learning. God maintained my faith in the deliverance which was to be an answer to my continual prayers to Him and the Virgin Mary (to whose intercession I am confident my deliverance is due).

Just such a character as the Moorish alchemist was described by Holmyard in his classic *Alchemy*, where a chapter is devoted to Holmyard's friendship with a 20th century

Moroccan adept. Such a person would *by definition* belong to one of the classical Sufi orders. If "St. Vincent" had turn'd Turke, he might have ended up in a Fraternity like the Shadhiliyya, where these occult mysteries are sometimes taught.

Note once again, in the St. Vincent text, the aura of *seduction* that hovers around the image of conversion: "...promise of wealth... all the secrets of his learning..." — and the "great love" the Moor feels toward Vincent. This almost seems an obligatory trope of the "captivity narrative" as a literary genre, and I would maintain that it illustrates my thesis of the "positive shadow" of Islam embedded secretly in the European discourse of religious and racial bigotry. Here is the intellectual equivalent of those "Moorish nieces". These texts are pregnant with an unspoken yearning, quite erotic in tone, to embrace the enemy of all Christendom. One is reminded of those other "captivity narratives" written by New England women and children who had been taken away by Indians. Not all of them wanted to return to civilization, and many actively resisted re-capture by Puritan husbands and fathers. They were quite happy—some of them—to "turn Indian" and escape from the Puritan patriarchy. Their narratives are likewise embued with a perfume of *seduction*.

Only a rare Renegado might be attracted to alchemy or Sufism, but Moroccan Islam knows other forms of mysticism, which might be called rural/non-literate in contrast to the urbane literacy of the Shadhiliyya. The "marabout orders" have been discussed at some length, usually by anthropologists rather than scholars of Sufism, and I won't attempt to explain them here. [See Geertz, 1968; Crapanzano, 1973.] A few broad themes should be sketched, however. These popular orders are frequently centered on the tomb of a saint and its attendant miracles—cures for disease, usually—but also (as we know) the stilling of ocean storms and blessings in the *jihad*, matters of great import to a corsair. Some of the orders are involved in more complex healing rites, which usually concern possession by *jinn* or spirits. As in the Tarantella, the symptoms of possession (paralysis, nervous disorder, hysteria, etc.) can only be alleviated by music and dance. Each djinn (like each "spider" in South Italy) has its own color, food, incense, rhythm, and dance. Some orders deal with particular jinn, like Aisha Qandisha (who appears to be a survival of the Phoenician/ Canaanite goddess Qadusha) or the goat-god, Boujaloud, celebrated and propitiated by the modern-day Master Musicians of Jajouka, and perhaps (according to Brion Gysin) a Moroccan survival of Pan himself [Gysin, 1964]. The usual way of joining such an order is to become possessed, so that one comes to depend on the ceremonies of the sect for one's very peace of mind and health. As with Voodoo, possession thus plays a positive as well as a negative role. The magical *experience of healing* provides existential "proof" of a magical world-view, and at the same time the communal nature of the experience creates group solidarity and reinforcement of social cohesion. Unlike the classical Sufi orders, the Marabouts and healing cults are popular, public, and highly visible. Since sailors are in fact notoriously "superstitious", we can assume that our Renegadoes would at least take an interest in the folk-magic aspect of the orders.

Another popular route toward mysticism in Morocco is the psychedelic path of *kif*, hashish, opium, datura, and other entheogenic plants. At least one Moroccan order, the Heddawiyya, are entirely devoted to the ritual, meditational, and magical uses of cannabis. Moroccan folklore preserves an atmosphere of bohemian abandon, intuition, dreaminess, surreal wit, cleverness, and *baraka* (spiritual power), in its depictions of *kif* users [Bowles, 1962]. And we might imagine how devastating the psychedelic experience would have

EUROPEAN RENEGADOES ENJOYING THEMSELVES

been for a European who knew only the dionysiac mystique of wine. Did the Renegadoes use cannabis? I think I have proof. In an engraving depicting "European Renegadoes Enjoying Themselves", from N. de Nicolay's *Les Quatres Premiers Livres de Navigations Orientales* (1568), we see three rogues dressed half-Turk half-European, which would suggest a setting in Algiers or Tunis; but we can extrapolate to Morocco. No wine bottles are in sight, yet the corsairs are floating along in a hilarious mood. One, in a dervish hat decorated with jasmine or some other flower, is about to eat something that looks like a sweetmeat. What else could it be but *majoun*, the famous North African concoction of hashish, nuts, fruit, honey, butter, etc., which Baudelaire and his comrades imitated so poorly with their mint-jelly confitures?

In discussing the religious life of Salé we must also note the important role of the Jewish community in the 17th century. The original Jewish population, which may date back to pre-Islamic times, called "the Settlers" (*Toshavim*), lived mostly in Old Salé in the *Mella* or Jewish quarter near the Maranid School of Medicine. Since 1492, however, the Cities of the Two Banks had seen the immigration of a whole new Jewish population, and the Spanish *Marranos* (nominal Christians like the Moriscos), and others from Iberia, called "the Exiles" (*mgurashim*), and a general influx of Sephardim and European Jewish merchants. With some exceptions Salé usually received the Jews with equanimity if not hospitality—although the "Settlers" apparently disliked the "Exiles" for their foreign ways and greater sophistication, just as the old-time Moors of Old Salé disliked the Moriscos. It's probable therefore that most of the newcomers settled in Rabat. Late in the 16th century, 400 widows expelled from Portugal arrived in Salé and brought with them their craft of embroidery in silver and gold thread. But most of the Jews were merchants (like the Rabbi who owned 1/6th of Sieur Mouette), some of them extremely wealthy and powerful—Brown mentions one Amran ben Hayut, whose gravestone proclaims him a Finance Minister. [Brown, 1971: 56]

I've found mention of only one Jewish corsair rais, working for Algiers, Sinan "the Jew of Smyrna", who was suspected of practicing magic because he was such an expert at navigation. [Gosse, quoted by Coindreau, 1948: 132] In fact Jews everywhere in the Islamic world, and especially in

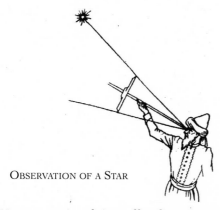

OBSERVATION OF A STAR

Morocco, enjoyed (or suffered) a reputation for magic. Up until the 1970's when many Jews left Morocco, a Moslem might well consult a Jew by preference in such matters as amulets and talismans, certain kinds of agricultural magic, love spells, etc. The Jew as "other" was seen as uncanny, both outside and yet inside society, inferior to "true believers" but somehow also supernaturally more gifted. But there may well have been other Jewish pirates, including some Renegadoes of Jewish origin. There exist sound reasons for such a supposition. Rabbi Y. Sasportas, a descendant of Maimonides, born in Oran, lived in Salé "for a good part of the 17th century. He later lived in Europe, but while at Salé he always had contact with and visitors from such far-flung places as Jerusalem, Livorno, Hamburg, Amsterdam; the Sultan of Morocco used him as an ambassador to the court of Spain." Sasportas was apparently the leader of those "Exiles" who embraced the teachings of the "False Messiah", Sabbatai Sevi. This enthusiasm proved one of the chief bones of contention between the "Exiles" and the "Settlers", since the latter group utterly rejected the former's messianic fervor. Sabbatai Sevi (also from Smyrna) claimed to be the Messiah, and taught a kind of antinominian Kabbalism—a

181

relaxation of the Law in favor of pure esotericism. The great G. Scholem has devoted one of his most precious and painstaking works to this movement so I need say little more about it—except to note that in the year 1666 (widely expected to mark the end of the world), the Messiah was arrested in Istanbul and *converted to Islam* [Scholem, 1973]. This act of apostasy caused most of his followers to desert him, but enough remained faithful to form a sect of nominal Moslems called *Donmeh* which still survives today in Turkey. Originally the sect had a wider distribution and may have included some of Rabbi Sasportas' congregation in Salé. After 1666, in the post-Republic era of piracy under the Alawite-Sharifian dynasty, Salé may well have enjoyed the services of Sabbatean Renegadoes.[36] In any case the mystical rabbis were frequently friendly with the mystical Sufis, and messianic/kabbalistic ideas were probably known and discussed outside the Jewish community. Sabbatai's ideas bore a close resemblance to those of various Protestant mystics and groups such as the Fifth Monarchy Men, who also embraced chiliastic dreams. The Revolution in England turned up countless mystical millenarians, including many from the working classes, and it would be quite legitimate (I believe) to assume that the Renegadoes were aware of such movements and beliefs. N. Cohn and C. Hill have demonstrated that the Millenium, and "the World Turn'd Upside Down", served not just as religious images but also and simultaneously as elements in a *revolutionary (proto) ideology* which used spiritual language to express political meanings and intentions. Levelling, destruction of the rich, the anarchy of the Ranters and the communism of the Diggers, were all

---

36. It's interesting to note that one of the few buildings in "New Salé" (Rabat) which can be dated to the "pirate era" is the borj of Sidi Makkluf, a patron-saint of sailors who was said to have been a Jewish convert to Islam. See Caillé, 1949: 275.

experienced *both* as mystical states *and* insurrectionary causes. I would propose that to some extent the Renegadoes can
be seen and interpreted in the light of this spiritual/political
ferment, in which social resistance invariably manifests in
some religious form. Sabbatai's apostasy might well have
been understood in Salé (and Barbary in general) as a kind
of vindication of the Renegado experience, or at least as an
esoteric deepening of its meaning. Islam, after all, is the most
recent of the three Western Monotheisms and thus contains
within it a revolutionary *critique* of Judaism and Christianity.
The apostasy of a self-proclaimed Messiah or of a poor
anonymous mariner would therefore invariably be seen as an
act of rebellion. Islam, to a certain extent, was the
Internationale of the 17th century—and Salé perhaps its only
true "Soviet". At first hearing Salé sounds a rather godless
place, a nest of riotous atheistical pirates—but the harder
one listens the more Salé seems to echo with long-ago voices
raised in excited debate or ecstatic preaching. The texts are
lost or perhaps never existed; it's an oral culture, an aural
culture...almost impossible to catch the last fading mur-
murs...but not *quite* impossible!

We began the story of Salé with a folktale about a corsair and a mermaid which points at the intense and rather
uncanny *erotic nature* of Moorish piracy. Such an eros must
invariably appear unnatural to those who "stay-at-home",
within their own cultural/moral universe, and never break
out into the spatial nomadism of the pirate or the psychic
nomadism of the heretic. We've already noted that Moorish
women were imagined (by such stay-at-home souls) as dangerous sorceresses, inhumanly beautiful and voracious. This
is interesting: the truth is that (for men at least) Islamdom
was a far more sexually-liberated culture than Christendom.
The Shariah allows both polygamy and concubinage, and it
allows divorce. The Prophet spoke several times in favor of

183

sexual pleasure, and Ibn 'Arabi (a major influence on Moroccan Sufis) writes in a highly tantric way of sexual pleasure as a form of mystical attainment. [See the chapter on Muhammad in Austin, 1980] On the popular level there can be no doubt that this pleasure–positive aspect of Islam has always seemed dangerously attractive to certain souls within Christendom, and we can be sure it motivated the Renegadoes. We can also be sure—because we are well-informed by such witnesses as the good Père Dan—that the widespread oriental custom of pederasty constituted an attraction for certain Renegadoes.

Homosexuality is of course just as forbidden in Islamic Law as in most other religious codes. But Christian society took a much more negative stance toward such practices than Islamic society. In North Africa, as elsewhere in Dar al-Islam, both the practice and the ideal of same-sex love was more "socialized" (to use a sociological catch-phrase) than in Europe. It was tolerated on the social level and highly valued on the ideal level—as we may well understand from the pederastic romanticism of so much Sufi poetry. To a certain extent one may even say it was institutionalized—despite the Shariah—as a recognized way of life. Père Dan recounts with pious disgust how boy-captives run the risk of becoming the "*mignons*" of debauched Moors and Renegadoes.[37] In Algiers—and in general—Jewish and Christian boys were often prefered as beloveds, in part because some social stigma attached to the passive partner and the virginity of Moslem boys was consequently better guarded, and in part because of the exotic beauty of Icelandic or Irish or Sephardic boys. Non-Moslem boys were more accessible—

---

37. Baker, the English Consul in Tripoli, "was fascinated by sexual conduct and mores that differed from his own, particularly by homosexuality, which, according to him, was quite acceptable in Tripoli..." See Pannell, 1989: 62.

sometimes as slaves—but could also be expected to "turn Turke" more readily than an adult captive. The great Albanian-born Renegade Algerian corsair Morat Rais (not to be confused with the Murad Rais of Salé) was given command of his first ship when he was 12 or 13, by a pirate captain who was infatuated with him to the apparent point of idiocy! (Morat however justified the Captain's lunacy by his instant success and subsequent brilliant career in piracy.)

Burg's *Sodomy and the Pirate Tradition* (1984) makes the very logical point that the generally all-male society of the pirates, freed of all law and conventional morality, must have seemed an obvious world of refuge for the persecuted homosexuals of 17–18th century Europe—especially for mariners, who were already known for such proclivities. Burg maintains that the normal homosexual pirate affair would involve adult men—i.e., "androphile" homosexuality. Unfortunately for this thesis Burg fails to document very many such relations, and has to take most of his actual examples from the ranks of boy-lovers instead. Here anecdotal and even archival evidence is plentiful. Burg however then goes on to stigmatize adult-youth relations as "pedophilia", a current term of clinical disapproval, tantamount to "child abuse". Burg, who implies that his sociological judgements are based on the ideology of "gay liberation" (which excludes boy-love from its roster of PC-ness), goes so far as to apply modern therapeutical categories to pirate pederasts, whom he accuses of "low self-esteem", "feelings of inferiority, immaturity, and passivity"; they suffered from "deep-seated feelings of inferiority or hostility toward their social superiors," etc., etc. According to Burg, the true pirate ideal was a "satisfying relationship between men."

Burg can be criticized, I think, for applying late-19th century categories to his analysis of the 17th and 18th century pirates. A Foucauldian history of sexualities would indicate that such phenomena as pederasty or androphile homosexuality are *behaviors* rather than *categories*. Seen as categories, such phenomena can only be called social constructs rather than natural states of being. The imputation of "normalcy" or the privileging of one sexual behavior over another is truly a double-edged sword for any homosexual theory, since these are precisely the terms used by heterosexual theory to discredit and condemn *all* same-sex love. In any case, the word "homosexual" belongs to the late 19th century, and the concepts of androphilia and pedophilia are even later refinements. The 17th century knew no such words, nor did it recognize any categories which might have been expressed in such words. It knew certain behaviors—it knew the love of two shipmates or *matelots* and it knew the love of a man and a youth, the captain and the cabinboy, the Moor and his *mignon*. In the Islamic world, sex and romance between two grown men was considered more unnatural than the love of a beautiful boy, which even the Prophet accepted as "natural" although "forbidden" (there are cup-bearers in Paradise as well as houris). Sufis praised boy-love, the Janissaries of Algiers practiced boy-love, and we may be sure that some Sally Rovers did so as well. Pederasty—not "andro-" or "pedophilia"—was a category known and widely accepted in Islamdom as "normal", despite Koranic injunctions. I will not attempt to prove that this was also the case for Burg's European pirates (he never discusses the Barbary corsairs), but *will* assert that it was the case in Salé-Rabat in the 17th century. As with the poets who flocked to Tangiers in the 1950's, we can feel sure that Morocco, even in the 1630's, was known as a refuge for men who love boys. But (unfortunately for the historian avid for texts!) they were not poets, but pirates.

IX

PIRATE UTOPIAS

And so, having followed our Corsairs' calendar through the social season—winter—we return to spring and the urge to set out once again roaming the open seas. I can't say that these scattered images of *Renegado culture* add up to anything like a hypothesis or a theory or even a very coherent picture. We've certainly had to use our imagination more than a "real" historian would allow, erecting a lot of suppositions on a shaky framework of generalizations, and adding a touch of fantasy (and what piratologist has ever been able to resist fantasy?). I can only say that I've satisfied my own curiosity at least to this extent: That something like a Renegado culture *could have existed*; that all the ingredients for it were present, and contiguous, and synchronic. Moreover, there exists good circumstantial evidence for this culture in what we might call its one great artifact—the Moorish Corsair Republic(s) of the Bou Regreg. Such an original concept would almost seem to depend on a *depth of origin* which can only be labelled "cultural", i.e., sociologically complex, and self-involved enough to be called (and to call itself) *different*. The Mafia names itself "Our Thing"; the corsairs called their "thing" the Republic of Salé—not just a pirate hang-out or safe harbor, but a pirate utopia, a planned structure for a corsair society. Perhaps a kind of *Franco* or lingua franca might have emerged in Salé as in Algiers, though we have no evidence for it. But Salé had its own language of signs and institutions, of relations and ideas, of goods and peoples, which clearly coalesced into some identifiable social entity. Exiles — whether Jews, Moriscos, or European rogues—created a crosscultural synergy (against a Moorish background) which can be identified as a new synthesis rather than simply a mishmash of styles. In our conclusion we shall try to analyze this culture as a *pattern of conversions*, of literal crosscultural adventures, of *translations*.

As a preliminary move in this analysis, it might prove interesting to compare the political structure of the Triple Republic with other political structures. Two obvious comparisons spring to mind—first, the other Barbary states, especially Algiers; and second, other "pirate utopias" elsewhere in the world.

We've already noted that although Algiers never really attained independence from the Sublime Porte, it managed to concoct a bizarre sort of freedom for itself out of the shouting-matches in the Divan of the *Ocak*, the connivances of the pirate *Taiffe*, the sheer cowardice of various Ottoman bureaucrats, and—if all else failed—the "democracy of assassination". The legislative structure of the Bou Regreg Republic was almost certainly modeled on that of the Algerian *taiffe*—in fact, at times the two bodies may have even shared members. But in Salé, the Taiffe ruled alone, as a Divan, without other power-sharing institutions as in Algiers. Apparently the Salé Divan, or rather Divans, were organized more democratically than the Algerian model. Grand Admirals were elected for one-year terms, as were the 14 or 16 captains of the assembly. Bureaucratic appointments were made—Customs and Excise, port officials, guardians of the peace (not a very efficient lot, one might surmise), etc.—but there was a clear and obvious intention to prevent political power from ossifying or even stabilizing to any significant degree. Clearly the Andalusians and corsairs liked to keep things *fluid*—even to the point of turbulence. All attempts to establish real control, at least in Rabat and the Casbah, were met with immediate violence.

May we surmise that this *autonomy* meant something more to the corsairs than merely a chance to maximize profits? In fact, was their brand of "perpetual revolution" really compatible with any serious proto-capitalist designs and ambitions? Wouldn't a monarchy (preferably a corrupt monarchy) have better served the purposes of simple fiscal aggrandizement? Isn't there something *quixotic* about the whole Bou Regreg phenomenon? With the possible exceptions of the Venetian or Dutch Republics of oligarchs, and the *Taiffe* of Algiers, the corsairs lacked any real-world models for their democratic experiment.[38] But the *idea* of a republic was very much in the air—and by 1640 would emerge into European history with the revolutions in England, then America, then France. Was it just an accident of history that all this should be preceded by the *Republic* of Salé? Or should we re-write the historical sequence to read: *Salé*, England, America, France? An embarrassing thought, perhaps: Moorish pirates and renegade converts to Islam as the hidden forefathers of Democracy. Better not pursue it.

Later in the 17th and early 18th century, a number of independent "pirate utopias" came into being elsewhere in the world. The most famous of these were Hispaniola, where

---

38. They might have known about the Uskoks, pirates who lived on islands off the Yugoslavian coast and preyed mostly on Moslem and Venetian shipping, and seem to have had a kind of egalitarian-tribal form of government. [See Bracewell, 1992]

the Buccaneers created their own short-lived highly anarchic society; Libertatia, in Madagascar; Ranter's Bay, also in Madagascar; and Nassau, in the Bahamas, which was the last classical pirate utopia.

Most historians have failed to note the significance of the pirates' *land enclaves*, seeing them simply as resting-places between cruises. The notion of a *pirate society* is a contradiction in terms in most theories of history, whether Marxist or otherwise — but the Buccaneers of Hispaniola (modern Santo Domingo) constituted just such a society. Hispaniola was a sort of No Go Zone in the late 16th or early 17th century; the Native population had declined, and no European power held an effective claim. Shipwrecked sailors, deserters, runaway slaves and serfs ("Maroons") and other dropouts began to find themselves in Hispaniola, free of all governance, and able to make a living of sorts as hunters. Feral cattle and pigs, descended from the herds of failed and vanished attempts at settlements, roamed the forest, along with wild game. *Boucan* or smoke-dried meat (a technique learned from the native Caribs) could be exchanged with passing ships for other merchandise. Here originated the "Brethren of the Coast", quite conscious of their freedom and organized (minimally and egalitarianly) to preserve it. Later communities were founded in Tortuga and New Providence. The Buccaneers turned only gradually to piracy, and when they did so they banded together under "Articles" or ships' constitutions, some of them quoted by Exquemelin (the only eye-witness chronicler of the Buccaneers in their "golden age"). The Articles are almost the only authentic pirate documents in existence. They generally called for election of all officers except Ship's Quartermaster and other "artists" such as sailmaker, cook, or musician. Captains were elected and received as little as one-and-a-half or two times a crewman's share. Corporal punishment was outlawed, and disagreements even between officers and men were resolved at a drumhead court, or by the Code Duello. Sometimes a clause would be inserted by some dour Welsh pirate (like "Black Bart" Roberts) forbidding women and boys on board ship — but usually not. Liquor was never forbidden. Pirate ships were true republics, each ship (or fleet) an independent floating democracy.

The early Buccaneers lived a fairly idyllic life in the woods, a life marked by extremes of poverty and plenty, cruelty and generosity, and punctuated by desperate ventures to sea in leaky canoes and jury-rigged sloops. The Buccaneer way of life had an obvious appeal: interracial harmony, class solidarity, freedom from government, adventure, and possible glory. Other endeavors sprang up. Belize was first settled by Buccaneers. The town of Port Royal on Jamaica became their stomping ground; its haunted ruins can still be seen beneath the sea that drowned it whole in 1692. But even before this quietus of biblical proportions the Buccaneer life had already come to an end. The brilliant Henry Morgan, bold and lucky, rose to leadership, organized the amazing Buccaneer invasion of Panama in 1671 — then took the Pardon along with an English appointment as Governor and High Judge, and returned to his old haunts as the executioner of his old comrades. It was certainly the end of an era; the surviving Buccaneers, cut adrift from permanent land bases, became *pirates*.

But the "golden age" dream lingered on: the sylvan idyll of Hispaniola became both a myth of origin, and a political goal. From now on, whenever the pirates had a chance, they would attempt the foundation of permanent or semi-permanent land enclaves. The ideal conditions included proximity to sea-lanes, friendly Natives (and Native women), seclusion and remoteness from all writ and reality of European power, a pleasant tropical climate, and perhaps a trading post or tavern where they could squander their booty. They were prepared to accept temporary leadership in a combat situation, but on shore they preferred absolute freedom even at the price of violence. In pursuit of booty, they were willing to live or die by radical democracy as an organizing principle; but in the enjoyment of booty, they insisted on anarchy. Some shore-enclaves consisted of nothing more than a hidden harbor, a beach where ships' hulls could be scraped, and a spring of clean water. Others were vicious little ports like Port Royal or Baltimore, run by "respectable" crooks like Thomas Crooke, who were simply parasites on piracy. But other enclaves can really only be called intentional communities—after all, they were intended, and they were communal—and therefore can rightfully be considered as *Pirate Utopias.*

In the early 1700's the scene of action shifted from the Caribbean to the Indian Ocean. Europe had begun its colonialist-imperialist relations with the "Near" East and India, but a great deal of territory remained "untamed". The perfect location for land-enclaves proved to be Madagascar, conveniently located near the Islamic pilgrimage sea route to Arabia and Mecca. The famous Capt. Avery established a legend by scoring the imperial Moghul dhow on its way from India to the Hajj, winning a diamond the size of an egg, and "marrying" a Moghul princess; the diamond and other jewels were reputedly buried somewhere around or in Boston Harbor and have never been recovered. Other pirates had no desire to return to either America or Europe, and Madagascar looked promising. Neither Islam nor Christianity had penetrated the huge island, which remained tribal, pagan, and even "megalithic" in its hundreds of Native "kingdoms". [For Megalithic practices in Madagascar, see Mohen, 1990: 55–58] Some tribes proved eager for alliances with the pirates, and some of the women too. The climate was ideal, a few trading posts were opened, and the concept of the Pirate Utopia was revived. In some cases an individual adventurer might "marry the king's daughter" or in some other way insinuate himself into Native society; in other cases a group of pirates would settle in their own village, near a friendly tribe, and work out their own social arrangements.

One such utopia was founded at "Ranter's Bay"—a place-name which, as C. Hill points out, lends some credence to the assumption that radical antinomian sects may have found adherents amongst the pirates [Hill, 1985]. According to Daniel Defoe's *The King of the Pirates* (1720), Capt. Avery himself settled for a while in Madagascar as a "mock-king". Hill points out that "Defoe stressed the libertarian aspects of Avery's settlement. 'In a free state, as we were, everybody was free to go wherever they would.'" [*ibid.*, p. 178] Another Madagascar settlement was made by one Capt. North and his crew. But without a doubt the most interesting and the most famous of the Madagascar utopias—certainly the most *utopian*—was "Libertatia" (or Libertalia).

Our only source for Libertatia and its founder Capt. Mission is a book written by Daniel Defoe, under the pen-name "Captain Charles Johnson", *The General History of the Pyrats* (1724–28). It is not a work of fiction, and a great deal of it can be supported by archival material, but it is clearly meant as a *popular* work, long on color and excitement, short on documentation. Defoe claimed to have derived all his information about Libertatia from a "Mission MS" in his possession. According to Defoe, this was the tale told by the manuscript:

Youngest son of an ancient Provençal family, Mission leaves home at 15 to study at the military academy at Angiers, then volunteers for service aboard a French man-of-war in the Mediterranean. While on leave in Rome he meets a "lewd" Dominican priest named Caraccioli who has lost his faith and decides to ship out with Mission. In a battle with a pirate, both are distinguished by their bravery. Gradually Caraccioli converts Mission to atheism and communism, or rather to "perfect Deism".

Then, in a fight with an English ship, the French captain and officers are killed. Caraccioli nominates Mission for the captaincy, and both men deliver long speeches to the crew, persuading them of their revolutionary designs (and mentioning Alexander the Great, Henry IV and VII of England, and "Mahomet", as figures of inspiration!). They persuade the crew to found a "new marine republic." "Every man is born free, and has as much right to what will support him as to the air he respires."

The bo'sun Mathew le Tonder suggests flying the black flag (the so-called Jolly Roger) as their standard—but Caraccioli objects, saying "they were no pirates but men who were resolved to effect the Liberty which God and Nature gave them." He makes reference to "Peoples' Rights and Liberties," "shaking the yoak of tyranny," the "misery of oppression and poverty." "Pirates were men of no principle and led dissolute lives; but *their* lives were to be brave, just, and innocent." For their emblem they choose a white ensign with the motto "For God and Liberty." (All this sounds more like *Deism* than "Atheism", but in the early 18th century the terms were still virtually interchangable.)

Mission and the crew now engage in a series of successful attacks on ships, taking as booty only what they need, then letting them go free. Episodes of chivalry and kindness alternate with courage and violence. Off the coast of Africa they capture a Dutch slaver; Mission makes another long speech to the crew, arguing "that the Trading for those of our own Species, cou'd never be agreeable to the Eyes of divine Justice. That no Man had Power of the Liberty of another; and while those who profess a more enlightened Knowledge

194

of the Deity, sold Men like Beasts; they prov'd that their Religion was no more than a Grimace!" Mission goes on to say that he, for one, "had not exempted his Neck from the galling Yoak of Slavery, and asserted his own Liberty, to enslave others," and he urges the sailors to accept the Africans as fellow crewmen—which they do.

Some time afterwards they settle down on the island of Johanna in the Indian Ocean, where Mission marries the daughter of "the local dusky queen," and the crew also find wives. For a few years Mission continues to make speeches, rob ships, and occasionally—when forced by circum-stances—to slaughter his enemies. (As Lord Byron put it, Mission "was the mildest manner'd man/ That ever scuttled ship or cut a throat.") [Quoted by Gosse, 1924: 218]

Mission now decides on a venture in intentional commu-nity, and moves his people to Madagascar.39 Here they begin to construct a purely socialist society in which private prop-erty is abolished and all wealth held in a common treasury. No hedges separate the pirates' plots of land. Docks and for-tifications are built, and two new ships, *Childhood* and *Liberty*, are sent to map the coast. A Session House is built, and Mission is elected "Lord Conservator" for a three-year term. The elected Assembly meets once a year, and nothing of moment can be undertaken without its approval. The laws are printed and distributed, as "they had some printers and letter-formers among them." The English pirate Capt. Tew is Admiral of the Fleet, Caraccioli is Secretary of State, and the Council consists of the ablest pirates "without distinction of nation or colour." A *new language* is invented, a mélange of French, English, Dutch, Portuguese, etc. This progressive

---

39. According to Course (1966), Libertatia was located near the NE tip of the island in Diego Suarez harbor or Antsirana.

régime fails to satisfy a few extreme radicals (including Capt. Tew), who break away to found their own settlement, based on pure anarchism—no laws, no officers. For a number of years (the Manuscript seems to have been vague about chronology) the Pirate Utopia flourished. When it finally fails it is not by fault of inner contradictions but of outside aggression: a tribe of unfriendly Natives attacks, the settlers put off to sea in their ships, and are destroyed by a freak hurricane.

Defoe himself lived during the last heyday of piracy, and much of his information derived from interviews with pirates imprisoned in London. A great many of his readers would have known a great deal about late 17th and early 18th century piracy, if only from news pamphlets and gallows ballads. As far as I can see, however, no contemporary reader ever questioned the reality of Capt. Mission. Despite the fact that Defoe's two chapters on Mission read like pages out of Rousseau—or Byron! (neither of whom were yet born)— and despite the fact that Libertatia's politics were in some ways far more radical than the politics of revolutionary America (1776) or France (1793)—or even Russia (1917), for that matter—despite all this, no one in 1728 blew the whistle on "Captain Johnson" or accused him of inventing Mission's story out of thin air. The material was believed, presumably, because it was *inherently believable*. Of course plenty of people believed in Lemuel Gulliver and Baron Munchhausen too; one cannot prove anything on the basis of popular belief; nevertheless, Capt. Mission was accepted as a fact until 1972.

In that year a new edition of the *General History* was prepared by Manuel Schonhorn (1972). In the introduction to this work, the reality of Capt. Mission was vigorously attacked on two main counts. First, negative evidence: no corroborating archival material exists (of course, it could have disappeared). Much more damning, however, was the problem of Capt. Tew. Plenty of archival and historical material exists on Tew, and there is no doubt of *his* existence — but the material shows that Tew could not have been in Madagascar long enough to carry out his role in the story of Libertatia. On this basis it was concluded that Mission's story is a *fiction*, a sort of Robinson Crusoe–type hoax, embedded in an otherwise historical (or more-or-less historical) text. The purpose of the hoax was to make radical Whig agit-prop. No "Mission MS" ever existed. Libertatia was a literal u-topia: it was "nowhere"!

We must admit that the Tew problem casts the Mission narrative in a somewhat apocryphal light; however, I believe that the verdict of nonexistence is forced and over-hasty. Several other logical possibilities should be considered: (a) Mission existed and the Manuscript existed, but contained misinformation about Capt. Tew (perhaps the name Tew was used to mask someone else), which Defoe uncritically accepted; (b) the Manuscript existed and described real events, but Defoe himself invented the episodes concerning Tew (including the "anarchist" schism) for reasons of his own, perhaps to flesh out a sparse narrative; (c) the Manuscript never existed, nor did any persons named Mission or Caraccioli — but some experiment like Libertatia actually occured in Madagascar, and was thinly fictionalized by Defoe (Robinson Crusoe had a real-life model in Alexander Selkirk, a genuine castaway survivor). "Johnson" added the name of a real pirate, Tew, to pump up the verisimilitude of the text, failing to realize that he was thereby giving the game away to future historians. None of these hypotheses can be proven or disproven on the basis of the Tew problem. Therefore the Revisionist Debunking Hypothesis — *complete fictionalization* — must also remain unproven. The mere passion for debunking should not be allowed to push us into abandoning the solid historicity of a *revolutionary hero* or a *real utopia*. [See, for example, the preface to Burroughs, 1981; also Law, 1980] Ranter's Bay was real enough, and so were the "Kingdoms" carved out in Madagascar by the "half-breed" children of the pirates. [See Deschamps, 1949, esp. pp. 215–229] The Buccaneers were real, and so were the wild crew at Nassau in the Bahamas (including Blackbeard, and "Calico Jack" Rackham and his two pirate wives, Ann Bonney and Mary Reade), which flourished for a few years in the early 1700's. Libertatia *could* have been real, and *should* have been real; this much will suffice for the admirers of Capt. Mission. Christopher Hill, for one, refuses to accept Mission as pure fiction. Hill points out that although Defoe was a fire-breathing radical as a youth, he had become a hack by the 1720's, and a supporter of bourgeois property values. "This is what makes the fairness of his description of Libertatia so remarkable. This would be surprising if he had invented the whole thing, less so if he had been listening to old sailors' tales and saw the possibility of using Libertatia to criticize aspects of capitalist society which offended him." [*op. cit.*, p. 179]

However, assuming for the sake of argument that the Mission chapters of the *General History* are at least as fictionalized as *Robinson Crusoe*, an interesting question arises. Defoe, it seems, knew rather a lot about the Republic of Salé. In the first few chapters of *Robinson Crusoe* the hero is captured by "Sally Rovers" and then taken to Morocco to be sold. As with St. Vincent de Paul and the Sieur Mouette, Robinson discovers that his Moorish master is not such a bad chap: he offers the English sailor a chance to escape slavery by converting to Islam. Crusoe, however, decides to attempt escape, and eventually succeeds in stealing a small boat. He is accompanied by a winsome young Morisco boy, with whom he shares no language—a clear foreshadowing of Friday, the beloved companion. *Defoe, it seems, could have used*

Salé as a partial model for Libertatia.

However, the comparison cannot be stretched too far. Salé was undoubtedly more libertarian than the Barbary Coast states of Algiers, Tunis, and Tripoli, but it certainly had far more conventional structure than any of the pure Pirate Utopias. The pirates of Salé clearly decided to accept a republican form of government (and the 10% tax) in order to safeguard their liberties on a (hopefully) permanent basis; Salé can be seen as a sort of compromise.

It would appear that they did this deliberately and consciously, although without any ideological/intellectual framework other than a hatred of European class oppression, and an admiration (or at least acceptance) of Islam. The so-called "democratic" aspects of Islam may have facilitated the emergence of Salé's unique experiment, but cannot fully account for it (since Islamic governments elsewhere were all monarchic). Protestant extremism (with its denial of all worldly "magistry" or government) may have been a factor—but not enough of a factor to save the Renegadoes from apostasy! Without any texts from Salé it's impossible to say for certain—but it looks as if the Bou Regreg Republic might have been the direct creation of the Andalusian Moriscos and European Renegadoes, with (perhaps) a bit of inspiration from certain Sufis—a genuine act of spontaneous political genius.

When the Renegadoes disappeared, they left behind them no "issue"—no obvious permanent trace of their existence. In Madagascar the pirates' "half-breed" children created a new culture, but in North Africa the converts and their descendants were simply absorbed into the general population. Their influence on European civilization seems to be nil, or even less than nothing: like relatives who have disgraced

199

themselves, they are not mentioned—not just forgotten, but deliberately forgotten. They did nothing to shift the border of Islamdom toward the West, despite their centuries of *jihad*. They created no distinctive art forms, and left behind not one page of "literature". A few names, a few anecdotes of cruelty…the rest has vanished. Despite the sheer anomalous mystery of their existence—thousands of 17th century European converts to Islam!—they have received almost no attention from analytical or interpretive historians; they have aroused no curiosity amongst historians of religion; they have faded to insignificance, almost to invisibility.

Pirates, apostates, traitors, degenerates, heretics—what positive meaning could possibly be expected to emerge from such a dire combination? Must we simply confess to a fascination with the perverse? After all, this constitutes the real motive of the piratologist, despite all protestations of shocked moral outrage, does it not? Not to mention the heresologist!

To answer this objection I would just point out (as indeed I've maintained elsewhere, e.g. Wilson, 1991, introduction) that heresy is a means of cultural transfer. When a religion from one culture penetrates another culture, it frequently does so (at least initially) as "heresy"; only later do the Orthodox Authorities arrive to straighten everyone out and make them toe the line. Thus, for example, early Celtic Christianity absorbed a great deal of Druidry, and was seen from Rome as "heretical". In the process, not only was Christian culture introduced into Ireland, but Celtic culture was also introduced (more surreptitiously) into Christianity, or rather, into Christian European culture. A cultural transfer occurred, and this cross-cultural synergy added up to something new—something which produced (for instance) the Book of Kells. Spain during the Moorish Era represents a culture based on three–way transfers amongst Islamic, Jewish, and Christian traditions, especially in such "heretical" fields as alchemy (or poetry!). Alchemy as a "heresy" transferred Greek science into Renaissance Christendom, via Islam. And so on, and so forth.

Apostasy can be considered as a special case of "heresy". And in the case of the Renegadoes, one very obvious area of cultural transfer consists of maritime technology. We can assume that not only did the Renegadoes introduce "round ships" and advanced metallurgy to Islamdom, they may also have introduced Islamic navigational mathematics and devices like the astrolabe to European mariners. This permeable boundary between "East" and "West" was most apparent in Moorish Spain, where mutual osmosis eventually generated a Columbus; and the process undoubtedly continued into the 17th century. We should be careful not to interpret this technical transfer as devoid of all spiritual significance — remember that Jewish Captain from Smyrna who was deemed a wizard for his navigational skills. The mariner's trade was a mystery, and the sailor (like the desert nomad) a man of suspect orthodoxy.

We have speculated that 17th-century mariners shared more than the secrets of a craft — they may have shared certain clandestine ideas as well: the idea of democracy, for example, or for that matter the idea of spiritual freedom, of freedom from "Christian Civilization" and all its miseries. If Islamophiliac notions circulated amongst educated Masons, why not also amongst a "masonry" of poor mariners? From ship to ship in whispers a rumor was circulated, a tale of the Barbary Coast, where wealth and "Moorish nieces" were to be won by the brave — by those few free spirits bold enough to renounce Christianity. If we have no written record of this "conspiracy", we may also ask what documents ever emerge from an oral and non-literate (sub)culture? We need no texts because we have proof of conspiracy in the otherwise-inexplicable historical fact of thousands of conversions, not only voluntary but emphatic; we have the evidence, in fact, of mass apostasy.

Here then we are given an example not only of heresy as a means of cultural transfer, but also (and even more interesting) heresy as a means of social resistance. And it is here (as I've already implied) that I find the "meaning" of the Renegadoes and their lost world. It's true that this theoria or "vision" of the pirates must be suspect as a prolongation of my own particular subjectivity—and even as a "Romantic" prolongation, to be sure. But it's also true that no subjectivity is entirely unique. If I make bold to interpret the Renegadoes' experience, it's because in some sense I recognize it. Every history comprises in some degree a "history of the present" (as Foucault says), and perhaps even more so, a history of the self. But "every history" is not therefore to be deemed devoid of "objectivity" or to be merely subjective and romantic.

I think I recognize the Renegadoes because somehow they too are "present". When Col. Qaddafi and the Irish Republican Army are accused of collusion and gunrunning, would it be misleading to mention the old, old Atlantean connection between Celts and North Africans? Just as the European Consensus of the 17th century denounced such conspiracy as treason and apostasy, so our modern media dismiss it as "terrorism". We are not used to looking at history from the terrorist's point of view, that is, from the point of view of moral struggle and revolutionary expropriation. In our modern consensus view, the moral right of killing and stealing (war and taxes) belongs only to the State; even more specifically, to the rational, secular, corporate State. Those who are irrational enough to believe in religion (or revolution) as a reason for action in the world are "dangerous fanatics." Clearly not much has changed since the 1600's. On the one hand, we have society; on the other hand, resistance.

The 17th century knew no such thing as a secular ideology. Neither States nor individuals justified their actions by philosophical appeals to science, sociology, economics, "natural rights", or "dialectical materialism". Virtually all social constructs were predicated on religious values, or (at least) expressed in religious language. As for the ideology of Christian monarcho-imperialism—or for that matter the ideology of Islamic piracy—we are free to interpret both as mere window-dressing, hypocritical verbiage, sheer hypocrisy, or even hallucination; but this is to reduce history to a psychology of rape and plunder, devoid of all thought and intention. The influence of "ideas" on "history" remains problematical and even mysterious—especially when we hypostatize such vague complexities as categories or even as absolutes; but it does not follow from this that we can say nothing meaningful about ideas or about history. At the very least we must admit that ideas have histories.

History has tended to view the Renegadoes' story as meaningless, as a mere glitch in the smooth and inevitable progress of European culture toward world domination. The pirates were uneducated, poor, and marginalized—and hence (it is assumed) they could have had no real ideas or intentions. They are seen as insignificant particles swept away from the mainstream of history by a freakish eddy or swirl of exotic irrationality. Thousands of conversions to the faith of the Other mean nothing; centuries of resistance to European-Christian hegemony mean nothing. Not one of the texts I've read on the subject even mentioned the possibility of intentionality and resistance, much less the notion of a "Pirate Utopia". The idea of the "positive shadow" of Islam is an ad hoc pro tem category I constructed in order to try to understand the enigma of apostasy; no historian (as far as I know) has ever posited a connection between the intellectual Islamophilia of Rosicrucianism and the Enlightenment, and the bizarre phenomenon of the Renegadoes. No one has

ever interpreted their conversion to Islam as a kind of ulti-
mate form of Ranterism, or even as a means of escape from
(and revenge upon) a civilization of economic and sexual
misery—from a smug Christianity based on slavery, repres-
sion, and elite privilege. Renegado apostasy as self-expres-
sion—mass apostasy as class expression—the Renegadoes as
a kind of proto-proletarian "vanguard": such concepts as
these have no existence outside this book, and even I hesitate
to advance them as anything more than quaint hypotheses.
The "vanguard" failed, the Renegadoes vanished, and their
incipient culture of resistance evaporated with them. But
their experience was not meaningless, nor do they deserve to
be buried in oblivion. Someone should salute their insurrectionary fervor, and their "temporary autonomous zone" on
the banks of the Bou Regreg river in Morocco. Let this book
serve as their monument; and through it let the Renegadoes
re-enter the uneasy dreams of civilization.

X

THE TROUBLESOME TURKE: A MOORISH PIRATE IN OLD NEW YORK

In Memory of Christopher Hill

Some years ago I went to the Main Branch of the New York Public Library in search of some book that would tell me all about "pirate utopias", pirate settlements on land. I failed to discover any such book. So far as I know there was then no such book. It seemed that if I wanted to read it some-one would first have to write it.

As it happens, the NYPL owns a huge number of books on piracy, most of them (at that time) squirrelled away in the 11th Avenue Annex. I did a bit of idle reading there, and put together a lecture on the subject for the Anarchist Forum (Libertarian Book Club) at the old Workmen's Circle in New York. The lecture was well received, but no one in the audience took up my challenge to write a book on pirate utopias. Years went by, I got tired of waiting, and decided to write it myself.

So I did. In 1995 Autonomedia published it.[40]

40. In the end I despaired of a complete treatment of the subject and decided to concentrate on one example—the Bou Regreg Republic—simply because no historian had ever thought of it as a

Some time later I was again wandering around the Main Branch when suddenly an unknown librarian tapped me on the shoulder and said, "Did you know that one of your Moorish corsairs ended up in New Amsterdam and was one of the first settlers in Brooklyn? He was called Anthony Jansen; you'll find him in the New York Genealogy Collection—because he had so many descendents. He was known as 'The Troublesome Turk'."

No. I hadn't known. I marvelled at the always-great librarianship of the 42nd Street NYPL. I promised to add a chapter to any future edition of *Pirate Utopias*. Here it is.

Anthony Jansen van Salee (or van Faes)[41] was born in Salé, Morocco, the son of Jan Janz a.k.a. Murad Rais, the amazing Dutch renegado who raided Iceland and Ireland and served as Grand Admiral of the Corsair Republic of Salé. Murad Rais had a Dutch wife and family, but also married an unnamed "Moorish princess" or "Spanish girl" after his apostasy. Anthony was clearly Murad's Moroccan child, since he was later called a "mulatto" in the New World. Anthony arrived in the Dutch colony of New Amsterdam on Manhattan Island a few years before 1638, when his name first appears in the records.

"pirate utopia". Vast amounts of research remain to be done even on Salé. Recent "pirate archaeology" in Belize may throw light on utopian communities there, but I know of no work in English on the "Pirates' Children" of Madagascar. In a book like this every footnote is a trap-door that drops the unwary reader into another whole world of bibliography — or of silence.

41. Presumably Anthony had lived for some time in both Salé and Fez.

Anthony was born sometime in the decade following 1600 (since he was said to be "about seventy" in 1669, and died in 1676). Murad Rais must therefore have visited or even settled in Salé before 1610 at the latest. Castries's *Sources inédites de l'histoire du Maroc* actually mentions Anthony's presence in Salé in 1623/4, by which time he would've been a young man. Therefore he would have been around 30 years old when he arrived in Manhattan; perhaps a few years older.[42]

By 1638 Anthony had already purchased a small farm in Manhattan and married Grietse Reyniers, a former barmaid from Amsterdam, a boistrous and quarrelsome woman. Anthony himself must have been rather daunting, not so much for his complexion but because he "was a man of great vigor...prodigious stature and strength" (even his descendents were said to be giants who performed feats of strength) and obviously quick-tempered. His manner was piratical, in fact.

42. This chronology presents certain problems in connection with dates given by Edmund Gosse for the life of Murad Rais. According to Gosse, Murad converted to Islam, settled in Salé, and married a "Spanish girl of fourteen" around 1618/9. If Anthony were born in 1619 he'd still be a teenager in the mid-1630s when he arrived in the New World, and only 57 when he died. But Gosse is a piratologist not an archival historian, and offers no documentation for his dating. It seems plausible to place Murad's conversion and marriage at some earlier date (and to interpret the word "Spanish" as "Morisco from Spain"). Perhaps the date 1600 is too early — but 1619 is too late. Murad was taken prisoner by the Knights of Malta in about 1632 and escaped only in 1640, by which time Anthony was in Manhattan, an adult with wife and babies. Indeed Anthony may have decided to emigrate from Salé because his father was gone and no longer Grand Admiral; the earliest date for Anthony's arrival in the New World would be about 1634, the latest would be 1637. Anthony could have been born around 1609/10 at the latest — otherwise the New World chronology simply makes no sense.

The newlywed couple burst into the New Amsterdam legal records with a rambunctious bang. In the years 1638/9 they were involved in fifteen of the 93 cases heard by the Courts, over 10% of the crime-rate. The Dutch of old Manhattan (about 2000 of them) devoted a huge amount of time to quarreling in Court, but the Jansens stand out even in such unruly company. Anthony's enemies called him a rascal and horned beast, and he was generally known as the Troublesome Turk (i.e., Moslem).

The Jansen van Salees made their legal debut in a case involving an unpaid debt to Domine Bogardus, concerning which Grietse accused the Domine of lying, and Anthony was quoted as saying, "If the Domine will have his money at once, then I had rather lose my head than pay him in this wise, and if he insist on the money, it will yet cause bloodshed."

Lysbert Dircks, a midwife called as a character witness, testified that she had assisted Grietse at her recent confinement. After the birth, Grietse asked Lysbert whether the baby resembled one Andries Hudden (a Council member, one of the gentry) or Anthony, her husband. The midwife replied dryly, "If you do not know who is the father, how should I know? However the child is somewhat brown."

The Jansens lost the case, and were soon in trouble again, Anthony for slander and Grietse for mooning the Fleet. Sailors of the Fleet had called out from shipboard to Grietse on shore: "Whore, whore two-pound butter whore!"—whereupon "she lifted up her petticoat and turning to the crew pointed to her behind," or slapped her backside and shouted, "*Blaes my daer achterin!*" To round off this portrait of Mrs. Jensen, other witnesses quoted her as saying (on another occasion), "I have long been the whore of the nobility; from now on I shall be the whore of the rabble!" The Jansens lost the case.

More cases followed: Anthony's hog killed someone's dog. Debts went unpaid. A pistol was waved about. Firewood was stolen. Drunkeness. Slander. More debt. Unsavory stories were told of Grietse's tavern-maid days in Old Amsterdam. In New Amsterdam "she pulled the shirts of some sailors out of their breaches and in her house measured the male members of three sailors on a broomstick." Finally it was too much for even the litigious colonials, and the Jansen ménage (now including several little girls) was exiled from Manhattan by order of the Court.

By today's standards they didn't go far — just to Brooklyn. But at the time Brooklyn scarcely existed, and they were the first non-Indian settlers in the Gravesend/ New Utrecht section of the future city. Anthony also owned land on Coney Island. He bought all the land from the Indians.[43] His estates were known as Turk's Plantation.

After a few years Anthony began showing his face in Manhattan again, and soon acquired property there as well. His farm prospered. Some of his family (eventually consisting of four grown and married daughters with children) settled in Brooklyn, some in Manhattan, and Anthony maintained his interests in both places. The fiery couple, the Turk and the barmaid, seem to have mellowed somewhat during their years of rustification, and gave up some of their more egregiously piratical mannerisms. Slowly they became gentry.

Perhaps not quite respectable gentry, however. Anthony doesn't disappear from Court records, although now most of the disputes concern property boundaries in Brooklyn. Anthony was kept busy sailing back and forth to Court in Manhattan, but now he sometimes won his lawsuits and cases.

43. According to the tribal maps of New York City in *Native New Yorkers* by Evan T. Pritchard (San Francisco, 2002), the area of Brooklyn where the Jansens settled was then occupied by the Canarsies, the Makeop, the Mocung and the Mannahaning.

Around 1669 Grietse died at Gravesend, and old Anthony remarried, a Manhattan widow named Metje Grevanraet. Anthony moved with her into a Manhattan house on Bridge Street (to be seen depicted in *Iconography of Manhattan Island*, a delightful collection of old maps and cityscapes.) By this time of course New Amsterdam had fallen to the English and become New York.

Metje may have been a Quaker; certainly she caused Anthony to be fined by the Court (the sum of one beaver) for harboring an English Quaker overnight at their house on Bridge St. (which was also at times run as an inn).

> April 16, 1674. Fragment of an affadavit setting forth that Samuel Forman of Oyster Bay came to the city where he lodged at the house of Anthony Jansen from Salee, and, by inspiration of Christ Jesus, intended to repair to the [Dutch] church during divine service and exclaim: "O cry wrath shall I cry, all flesh is grass, grass is the flower of the field, the flower falls and the grass withers but the word of God Obeids [abides] forever." — *Calendar of Historical Manuscripts in the Office of the Secretary of State* (Albany), XXIII/2/331

This case raises the question of Anthony Jansen's religion. He and his first wife Grietse were not known for piety and churchliness; it seems that Anthony was assumed to be a Moslem, a "Turk". Since he had grown up in Morocco this would appear likely enough. Later in his life he apparently conformed to the Dutch Church, and even petitioned (unsuccessfully) for a minister to be sent out to Gravesend. But in his youth Anthony might have been influenced by sufism, and certainly by the rough spirit of toleration and radicalism amongst the Renegadoes. He and his second wife might well have entertained Quakerish notions. In this context it's interesting to note that Jansen's nearest neighbors in Brooklyn after 1643 consisted of a small colony of English Anabaptists led by the eccentric Lady Deborah Moody, expelled from Plymouth Bay Colony for heresy. Lady Moody was a friend of Gov. Stuyvesant, and Jansen was on good terms with her.

Anthony brought a few precious items with him from Morocco: an engraved brass tray and "tea kettle", and a copy of the Koran. He was illiterate in Dutch and English; he signed depositions and deeds with his "mark":

This is the mark made by the own hand of ANTHONI JANSEN VAN FES.

but he may have been literate in Arabic. This Koran—perhaps the first in the New World—was passed down in the Van Sicklen and Gulick families, descended from Jansen, till in about 1886 it was sold to one Richard M. Johnson "for a trifling sum". (Johnson may himself have been a descendent of Jansen's as well, since the family had changed their name to this English spelling.) Johnson later sold it to an old Jewish dealer in Trenton known as "Jerusalem". Johnson had no idea what the book was, but Jerusalem recognized it and offered $50 for it. Johnson received only $25 however, because the dealer died before making the second payment. At this point the Koran disappears from view and is lost to history.

Anthony Jansen van Salee lived out his last years in Bridge St. and died in March, 1676. His second wife survived him by ten years, and lived in the house till her death.[44]

"Turk" and "Moor" were used in 17th-century European languages not always to designate inhabitants of Turkey and North Africa, but sometimes as synonyms for "Moslem". (Thus the Spanish called Moslems of the Phillipines "Moors", *Moros*.) In this sense we could say there's something "Moorish" about New York and we could read the story of Anthony Jansen as the first chapter of a book that might be called *The Secret Moorish History of New York*. This book has yet to be written. But for the benefit of anyone who might take on the task, here are a few chapters it might contain:

Although the Dutch probably owned slaves from Moorish parts of Africa they also brought a "Moorish" Prophet's image to New Amsterdam, namely, one of the Bible's Three Orient Kings (or Magi) — Caspar — who appeared blackfaced and turbanned in Dutch Yuletide Nativity skits.

Jansen probably wasn't the first pirate in old New York and certainly wasn't the last. Under English rule the city became one of the great pirate havens — although never a pirate utopia.[45] Anthony himself lived to see the rise of

44. Sources: Leo Hershkowitz, "The Troublesome Turk: An Illustration of Judicial Process in New Amsterdam", *New York History*, XLVI/4/Oct, 1965. Charles A. Hoppin, *The Washington Ancestry and Records of McClain Johnson & Forty Other Colonial American Families* (Greenfields,1932); Berthold Fernow, ed., *Records of New Amsterdam, 1653–1674* (New York, 1897); I.N.P. Stokes, *Iconography of Manhattan Island* (New York, 1895–1928)
45. It seems incorrect to accuse modern corporations of "bio-piracy" (the patenting of natural DNA, etc.) or to think of Capitalism

big-time piracy in New York, but by then most pirate voyages no longer focussed on the Mediterranean, nor even the Caribbean, but the Indian Ocean. Madagascar and the Malabar Coast of India were teeming with pirates; big prizes were won from Mughal shipping. New York's role was largely economic: expeditions were planned and financed, booty was fenced. Manhattan gentry families such as the Livingstones were deeply implicated. The disaster of Capt. Kidd's anti-pirate cruise in 1699 caused fear and trembling in New York halls of power, and Kidd was sent to London for hanging as a sacrifice to Whig political and financial interests.

During the late 17th and into the 18th century New York would have been touched by exotic cultures from Africa, North Africa, Madagascar and India. Many Malagasy slaves ended up in Manhattan. They're mentioned in accounts of the slave/Indian/Irish St. Patrick's Day Rebellion in the city in 1741. As far as I know, little research has been devoted to them.

America had close relations with North Africa immediately after independence: Morocco its first diplomatic partner, and Tripoli its first foreign war-enemy. A sailor in the U.S. Navy, a New Yorker named William Ray, was taken prisoner by the corsairs of Tripoli in 1803 and later wrote a block-buster account of his captivity, *The Horrors of Slavery* (1808). Ray rather admired the exotic and dashing enemy. As a radical freethinker in the Paine/Jefferson mode, he saved his sharpest criticisms for the U.S. Navy, and caused some scandal with his intemperate rhetoric. Ray retired to a

in general as piratical. Citicorp and Monsanto operate under the flags of nations, whereas pirates were "at war with all the world" and its rulers. Piracy may have helped fuel the rise of modern Capitalisms, but the pirates themselves cannot be be called proto-capitalists. In relation to banks and corporations it might be more accurate to speak of "privateering".

village upstate, Auburn, where he became a poet and cracker-barrel *philosophe*.

New York's greatest Moorish fad was sparked by Washington Irving's trip to Spain, where he fell under the spell of vanished splendor. *Tales of the Alhambra* (perhaps the first American world-class book) was followed by a *Life of Mohammed* and other Islamophilic works. Irving's companion and secretary on the Spanish voyage, Jay Wray Mould, took up architecture and collaborated with F. Law Olmsted on Central Park; Mould designed the beautiful Mauresque arcade around the Central Fountain. Mooromania became one of the established themes of American Romanticism—at least in New York. The poet, journalist, traveler and hashish afficionado Bayard Taylor promenaded on Broadway dressed in robe and turban. The artist Frederick Church built a Moorish palazzo called Olana in Columbia Co., with views of the Hudson and the Catskills, thus joining Luminism, Romanticism and Orientalism to produce a "Hudson River School."

In the 1850s New York artist/journalist and Freemason Albert Rawson travelled in the Orient where he met the young and beautiful Helena Blavatsky and had an affair with her. Rawson was (he claimed) adopted by the Bedouin, initiated by the Druzes, made sufi connections in Turkey, and met the great Algerian Shaykh and sufi mystic, Emir Abd al Qadir, who was also a Mason. Rawson and Blavatsky experimented with hashish. After their return to New York Blavatsky founded the Theosophical Society (based largely on Egyptian mysteries), and Rawson founded the Masonic Nobles of the Mystic Shrine—the "Shriners". The remarkable charter document of this fraternity claims authority from Turkish Freemasons, the Grand Sharif of Mecca, and the Bektashi Sufi Order.

Rawson and Blavatsky in turn influenced a remarkable Afro-American autodidact, Paschal Beverley Randolph, who used hashish spiritually and claimed initiation in Sex Magic by the Syrian Nusayris, an extreme Shiite sect. Randolph disseminated his teachings in self-published pamphlets and mail-order initiations.

Another Afro-American influenced by Rawson and Blavatsky was Timothy Drew, a former railroad porter and circus magician who named himself Noble Drew Ali, claimed initiation in the Great Pyramid of Egypt and authority from the Sharif of Mecca, and founded the Moorish Science Temple of America in Newark, New Jersey, in 1913. Many of Noble Drew's rituals were based on those of the Black Shriners, an offshoot of Rawson's Order, and his book, the *Circle Seven Koran*, contained large portions of a Theosophical work, *The Aquarian Gospel of Jesus*.

Moorish Science proved very popular in Brooklyn, and in fact today the plaza of a rundown crime-ridden housing project there is named after Noble Drew. Anthony Jansen was the first Moor of Brooklyn but not the last. America's first Sunni mosque occupies an old brownstone in Brooklyn on Greene St. off Atlantic Ave., founded in the 1920s by Yemeni sailors. Perhaps the local African Americans who began attending it had old family traditions of Islamic ancestry. Nowadays Brooklyn has scores of mosques, and not just in the old "Arab" neighborhood of Atlantic Avenue. And American Islam has its own martyred saint, Malcolm X, who died in New York.

The first edition of Pirate Utopias proved a fairly popular book. It won a mysterious "Rum & Sodomy" Award. It was translated into Hungarian (very elegantly, I'm told), and also appeared in a splendid big French version with lots of color illustrations. I'm pleased by this chance to add the chapter on "A Moorish Pirate in Old New York." I hope some day, to see the book translated and published in Arabic — Inshallah!

May 2003

BIBLIOGRAPHY

Abun-Nasr, Jamil M. (1971) *A History of the Maghrib.* Cambridge [U.K.]: Cambridge University Press

Ali, Ahmed and Ibram Ali. No date. *The Black Celts: An Ancient African Civilization in Ireland and Britain.* Cardiff: Punite Publications

al-'Arabi, M. (1980) *The Bezels of Wisdom (Fusus al-hikam)*, trans. and introduction R. W. J. Austin. New York: Paulist Press

Az-Zirr and A. N. Durkee, trans. (1991) *The School of the Shadhdhuliyyah*, vol. I, Orisons. Alexandria [Egypt]: Daru'l-Kutab

Barnby, H. (1969) "The Sack of Baltimore" in *The Journal of the Cork Historical and Archaeological Society.* Cork [Ireland], part 2–Vol. LXXIV, no. 220, July-Dec.

Birge, J. K. (1937) *The Bektashi Order of Dervishes.* London: Luzac

Bowles, Paul (1962) *A Hundred Camels in the Courtyard.* San Francisco: City Lights
    (1975) *The Oblivion Seekers and Other Writings.* San Francisco: City Lights

Bracewell, C. W. (1992) *The Uskoks of Senj: Piracy, Banditry and Holy War in the 16th Century Adriatic.* Ithaca: Cornell University Press

216

Brown, Kenneth (1971) "An Urban View of Moroccan History: Salé 1000-1800" in special issue of *Hespéris Tamuda*. Faculté des Lettres, Université Mohammed V. Rabat: Editions Techniques Nord-Africaines

Burroughs, W. S. (1981) *Cities of the Red Night*. New York: Holt, Rinehart and Winston

Caillé, J. (1949) *La Ville de Rabat jusqu'au protectorat Français*. Paris: Vanoest

Carteret, Sir George (1929) *The Barbary Voyage of 1638*. Philadelphia, Wm. F. Fell Co.

Chambers, Anne (1979) *Granule: Life and Times of Grace O'Malley*. Portmannock [Ireland]: Wolfhound Press.

Chimenti, Elisa (1965) "The Legend of El-Minar" in *Tales and Legends of Morocco*. New York: Ivan Obolensky

Cohn, N. (1970) *In Pursuit of the Millenium*. London: Maurice Temple Smith

Coindreau, Roger (1948) *Les Corsairs de Salé*. Paris: Societé d'Editions Géographiques, Maritimes et Coloniales

Course, A.G. (1966) *Pirates of the Eastern Seas*. London

Crapanzano, Vincent (1973) *The Hamadsha: A Study in Moroccan Ethnopsychiatry*. Berkeley: University of California Press

Deschamps, Hubert (1949) *Les Pirates à Madagascar aux XVIIe et XVIIIe siècle*. Paris: Editions Berger-Levreiul

Dunton, John (1637) *A True iovrnall of the Sally fleet, with the proceedings of the voyage*. London, printed by I. Dawson for T. Nicholes

Drinnon, Richard (1972) *White Savage: The Case of John Dunn Hunter*. New York: Schocken

Eberhardt, Isabelle (1987) *The Passionate Nomad: The Diary of Isabelle Eberhardt*. Trans. N. de Voogd. London: Virago

Eloufrani, Mohammed Esseghir ben Elhadj ben Addallah (1889) *Nozhet-Elhadi: Histoire de la dynastie Saasienne au Maroc*, Trad. Fran. par O. Houdas. Paris: Ernest Leroux

Ewen, C. L'Estrange (1939) *Captain John Ward, "Arch Pirate"*. Paignton: printed for the author.

Exquemelin, A. O. (1699) *The True History of the Bucaniers of America; from their first opriginal down to this time*. London: T. Newborough

Fernow, Berthold, ed. (1897) *Records of New Amsterdam, 1653–1674*. New York: Knickerbocker Press

Fuller, Basil and Ronald Leslie-Melville (1985) *Pirate Harbours and Their Secrets*. London: Stanley Paul & Co.

Friedman, Jerome (1987) *Blasphemy, Immorality, and Anarchy: The Ranters and the English Revolution*. Athens [Ohio]: Ohio University Press

Geertz, Clifford (1968) *Islam Observed: Religious Development in Morocco and Indonesia*. New Haven: Yale University Press

Gysin, Brion (1964) "The Pipes of Pan". *Gnaoua* 1:19-23. Tangiers [Morocco]

Hershkowitz, Leo (1965) "The Troublesome Turk: An Illustration of Judicial Process in New Amsterdam", *New York History*, XLVI/4/Oct, 1965

Hill, Christopher (1978) *The World Turn'd Upside Down*. London: Penguin
    (1985) "Radical Pirates". *The Collected Essays of Christopher Hill* Vol. 3: 161–187. Amherst: University of Massachusetts Press.

Hoppin, Charles A. (1932) *The Washington Ancestry and Records of McClain Johnson & Forty Other Colonial American Families*. Greenfield, O.: privately printed

Ibn al–Sabbagh, M. (1993) *The Mystical Teachings of al–Shadhili (Durrat al–asrar wa tuhfat al–abrar)*, trans. Elmer H. Douglas. Albany: State University of New York Press

Joyce, Cecily (1990) *Claddagh Ring Story*. [Galway. Ireland?]

Jullien, Philippe (1971) *D'Annunzio*. Paris: FayardLaw, Larry (1980) *Mission and Libertatia*. London: Spectacular Times

Lemprière, W. (1791) *A Tour from Gilbralter to Tanger, Sallee, Mogador, Santa Cruz, Tarudani, and Thence over Mount Atlas to Morocco: including a particular account of the royal harem*. (In Pinkerton, John, *A COllection of the best and most interesting voyages...* London, 1808–14)

Lloyd, C. (1981) *English Corsairs on the Barbary Coast*. London: Collins

Lucie-Smith, E. (1978) *Outcasts of the Sea*. New York and London: Paddington Press

Mohen, J. P. (1990) *The World of Megaliths*. New York: Facts on File

Morton, A. L. (1970) *The World of the Ranters: Religious Radicalism in the English Revolution*. London: Lawrence and Wishart

Norris, Gerald (1990) *West Country Pirates and Buccaneers*. Wimborne [U.K.]: Dovecote

Pannell, C. R. (1989) *Introduction to Piracy and Diplomacy in 17th Century North Africa: The Journal of Thomas Baker, English Consul in Tripoli, 1677-1685*. Rutherford [UK]: Fairleigh Dickinson University Press; Cranbury [NJ]: Associated University Presses

Penz, Charles (1944) *Les Captifs Francaise du Maroc au XVIIe siecle*. Rabat: Imprimerie Officielle

Pritchard, Evan T. (2002) *Native New Yorkers*. San Francisco: Council Oak Books

Quinn, B. (1986) *Atlantean: Ireland's North African and Maritime Heritage*. London: Quartet

Rediker, Marcus B. (1987) *Between the Devil and the Deep Blue Sea: Merchant Seamen, Pirates and the Anglo-American Maritime World, 1700-1750*. Cambridge [U.K.]: Cambridge University Press

Scholem, Gershom (1973) *Sabbatai Sevi: The Mystical Messiah*. Princeton: Princeton University Press

Senior, C. M. (1976) *A Nation of Pirates: English Piracy in its Heyday*. New York: Crane Russack

Smith, Nigel, ed. (1983) *A Collection of Ranter Writings from the 17th Century*. London: Junction

Les Sources Inédites de L'Histoire du Maroc (1935), ed. H. de. Castries. Tome III ed. P. de Cenival and P. de Cossé Brissac

Spencer, William (1976) *Algiers in the Age of the Corsairs*. Norman [OK]: University of Oklahoma Press

Stokes, I.N.P. (1928) *Iconography of Manhattan Island*. New York: R.H. Dodds

Westermarck, E. (1926 [1968]) *Ritual and Belief in Morocco*. New Hyde Park [NY]: University Books

Wilson, Peter Lamborn (1993) "Caliban's Mask" in Sakolsky, Ron and James Koehnline, eds., *Gone to Croatan: The Origins of American Drop-Out Culture*. New York: Autonomedia

Wolfe, J. B. (1979) *The Barbary Coast: Algeria and the Turks*. New York: W. W. Norton.